The Gift Part Two
The Air Force Years
By
Mike Trahan

ISBN-13: 978-1517210014

ISBN-10: 1517210011

3rd Edition
William Collins Publishing, London

Prologue

After flying for eight and a half years during high school and college, and participating in the Air Force ROTC Program at Ole Miss and The University of Texas, I felt I was well prepared for U. S. Air Force Undergraduate Pilot Training.

In October 1965, I became a member of UPT Class 67C at Webb Air Force Base in Big Spring, Texas. I can say, without reservation, that my year in UPT was the best year of my life!

After graduation from Webb I was assigned the C-141 Starlifter jet transport aircraft. I went to C-141 Transition Training at Tinker Air Force Base in Oklahoma City, Oklahoma in November of 1966. Afterward, I was assigned to the 76th Military Airlift Squadron at Charleston Air Force Base in Charleston, South Carolina. I flew the C-141 for two years.

In December 1968, I was ordered to go to Vietnam. My aircraft assignment was the AC-47 "Spooky" Gunship. I flew "Spooky" for eight months and was then reassigned to the EC-47 Electronic Countermeasures aircraft. I completed my one-year tour in that aircraft.

When I returned home after my Vietnam tour, I separated from the Air Force and started looking for an airline job.

Dedication

To my wife Sheila Joyce Trahan
Our Daughter Theresa

And

To the Magnificent Men and Women in The United States
Air Force (Past & Present)

Chapter 1

USAF Undergraduate Pilot Training

This was it! I had been working for this moment since I was fifteen years old. So many twists and turns had frustrated the way here, and some were maddening delays and roadblocks I thought I would never get past. But, that was all over now. USAF Undergraduate Pilot Training now stood before me. I was here!

We had all day to report in on October 22, but I was so eager to get started, I was at the base at 0900. As I approached the Main Gate, an Air Policeman motioned for me to stop. He said, "May I see your identification and orders Sir?" After he checked those items, I asked him where new students were supposed to check in. He told me to go to the Student Squadron (STURON) Building and gave me a map with directions how to get there. As I started driving away, he gave me a snappy salute, which I promptly returned. Damn, that felt good!

I drove straight to the STURON building. With orders in hand, I marched in and said, "Lieutenant Trahan reporting for duty!" A few snickers erupted from the enlisted people behind the desk, but they quickly recovered and processed me in. They said to be at the Base Auditorium at 0800 the next morning for Orientation.

My next stop was base housing. When I checked in, there was another new Second Lieutenant standing at the counter. We were both bachelor officers. The housing clerk took a look at our paperwork, got a sly grin on his face, and said, "I think you guys would be perfect roommates. You have a lot in common. Both of you went to college in Texas. One of you went to The University of Texas and the other to Texas A&M. I wondered if that guy knew what bitter rivals the Longhorns and the Aggies are. At least the Air Force had a sense of humor - a diabolical sense of humor!

My Roommate Jim Roberts

I turned to the other guy, stuck out my hand and said,

"Hello, I'm Mike Trahan from West Orange, Texas." He put out his hand and said, "Howdy, James Roberts from San Antonio!" James Montgomery Roberts walked into my life that day. He was my first and only Aggie roommate!

The clerk said, "Gentlemen, your BOQ apartment is not quite ready. Base Housing is doing some painting and renovating in that building right now. It should be ready in a few days, and it's going to be real nice when it's finished. I am going to house you temporarily at a motel down the street. Sorry, but it can't be helped." We said we didn't mind, but we really did.

A pretty good crowd had gathered when Jim Roberts and I arrived at the Base Auditorium at 0740 the next morning, Class 67C was coming together for the first time. We didn't know at the time that this would become one of the most spirited, industrious classes to ever grace the hallways of Webb AFB, a collection of recent college graduates and brand new Second Lieutenants from all over the United States.

While we milled around outside I started checking out the other guys in the class, scouting the competition so to speak. I expect every other man there was doing exactly the same thing. We all knew, even before we got there, that assignments were based on class rank at the end of the year, and we also knew it was a very competitive program. One guy caught my eye. I thought he looked more like the stereotypical jet pilot than any of us did. For all I knew, he could have been the leader of the Thunderbirds! I made a mental note to self: *"Keep an eye on this guy. He looks pretty sharp!"* I later learned his name was Emmons F. "Fred" Parrott. Time would later prove that my intuitions about Fred were correct.

We filed into the auditorium at 0750 and took our seats. I'll never forget the scene before me. The auditorium was big enough to seat around five hundred people. There were probably a hundred in there that morning. There was a large mural backdrop on the stage. It had a deep blue background and two airplanes depicted on it - a T-37 on the right and a T-38 on the left. The words LEARN and LIVE were written in bold print across the bottom of the mural. That not-too-subtle message was not lost on any of us.

The Vice Wing Commander gave the welcoming speech. We learned that Colonel August F. Taute, the current Wing Commander, had been killed in a car accident the week before we got there. Afterwards, Base Commander Colonel Franks said a few words. He then turned the podium over to the 3560th Student Squadron Commander, Lieutenant Colonel Bary Butler.

Colonel Butler was the perfect man for the job. He actually looked more like a Marine Drill Sergeant than an Air Force Officer: short and stocky, with a great flattop haircut, and all business. He told us our class consisted of sixty-five individuals from dozens of colleges. Three of us were foreign students: two from Morocco and one from Iran. We were members of the 3561th Student Squadron, and we would be divided into two sections - The 60th and 61st. Captain Wincie Daniels was the Tactical Officer for the 60th, and Captain William Picking was the 61st TO. The Tactical Officer's job was to guide the class through their year in UPT. They made sure we were always where we were supposed to be. Each section would have a student leader. The leader would be selected either by rank, or in the case of a section of equal rank, he would be chosen by the Tactical Officer.

Captain Bill Picking – 3561ˢᵗ Section T.O.

Colonel Butler told us UPT was a golden opportunity for all of us and that only a select few were chosen to be there. By the time we had finished our training, the Air Force would have invested a million dollars in each of us, and then he gave the most sobering statistic of all.

"Men, the attrition rate at UPT has averaged thirty-three percent over the last ten years. That will probably hold true for this class too. That means that every third person in your class will wash out. Work hard so that doesn't happen to you."

The next up to speak was Cal Lowry, a civilian. Everyone called him Coach Cal, because he was in charge of our daily Physical Training (PT) while we were at Webb.

"Men, flying these jets can be strenuous on the human

body. The better shape you are in, the better you will tolerate it, especially the G forces you will encounter on a daily basis."

I liked Coach Cal right away.

When Coach Cal finished talking, Captains Daniels and Picking took the podium. Daniels said, "The following men will be in the 60th Section," and he called out the names of about half of our classmates. Then Picking read his list. The rest of us were in the 61st Section. Jim Roberts and I were in the same section. That was fortunate for us as roommates because each section would operate on opposite schedules. If the 60th flew in the morning, then the 61st would be in Academics and vice-versa. They told us to be at the auditorium at 07:45 the next morning to board the busses to the Infirmary for our physicals.

We spent the remainder of the morning taking a guided tour of the base. We were shown the Academics Building, the Physical Training Building, gym and athletic fields, the Officer's Club where we would eat all our meals, the Infirmary, and other places we would frequent while there.

Our last stop was the Base Personal Equipment Shop where we were issued our flight gear: Flight suits, helmets, oxygen masks, parachutes, flight boots, computers, plotters, aircraft operating manuals, check Lists, and a nice brown leather briefcase to carry our books in. We each got four flight suits, one light flight jacket and one heavier winter flight jacket. I was proud that a medium-regular flight suit fit me perfectly! We were also issued an official grey Air Force watch with leather band and a cool pair of aviator sunglasses. We liked the sunglasses best of all!

When we got back to the auditorium we were dismissed for lunch. We were told to go to the Officers Club for a complimentary welcoming lunch. After that, we would pay for all our meals. Jim and I loaded our equipment in my GTO and drove over to the club. The place was teeming with men in flight suits. Some were Instructor Pilots (IP's), but most were students from the eight different classes that were going through training at that time. Approximately every six weeks a class would graduate, and a new class would come in and take its place.

Lunch conversation was pretty animated. We were all busy meeting each other and asking the obvious questions – Where are you from? What school did you go to? Are you ROTC, Officer Candidate School, or National Guard? Only one of our classmates, Paul Baker, was from the Air National Guard.

After lunch, we went back to the auditorium. We were told that the first phase of our flight training would not take place on the base. We would get that at Howard County Airport. Air Training Command had initiated a new program that year. Only two classes had gone through it before us. It was called the T-41 Program. ATC had discovered by the time a student was eliminated in the T-37 program, the Air Force had already invested about three hundred thousand dollars in him. The T-41 was a Cessna 172 that had been designed just for the Air Force to cheaply weed out those who did not have the aptitude to fly. My first Air Force airplane would be one that I had been flying for eight years and had over four hundred fifty hours in. Not only that, thanks to Glen Doss and the T-41 Flight Manual he gave me, I already knew all the maneuvers I would be doing in that airplane. My confidence level shot up a few notches.

At the end of the day we were dismissed. I had spent the day immersed in Air Force stuff, and it was a letdown to have to go spend the night at that motel again.

My flight physical went pretty well except for one thing. The airman that took my height and weight listed me as obese. However, the doctor quickly read him the riot act.

"This man is obviously an athlete. His BFI (Body Fat Index) is probably lower than yours. He is NOT obese!"

The doctor commented on the now repaired pilonidal cyst on my tailbone. He asked me how long it had been since that surgery, and I told him two years and two months. He said, "That is going to give you some problems when you start pulling serious G forces, but that won't happen until you get into the T-38, so it should be okay by then.

We all passed our physicals, and now we were all set for a glorious year dedicated to nothing but flying some pretty damn hot airplanes!

The rest of that day and the next one were spent going through more orientations and briefings. The two Section

Leaders were announced. Captain Tom Kelly was the obvious choice for the 60th Section. He was their ranking man. Tom was a former Navigator who had come back to go through pilot training. My section leader was Second Lieutenant David Kinton. Captain Picking selected him.

Chapter 2

The T-41 Program

T-41

At 0700 on the morning of October 25, my section boarded a bus bound for Howard County Airport to begin our flight training in the T-41 aircraft.

The T-41 Instructors were all civilians under contract to the Air Force. The Air Force owned the fleet of about twenty modified Cessna 172s. The only real difference I could see between this 172 and the one I flew in Orange was it didn't have a back seat.

One of the Air Force Instructor Pilots oversaw the T-41 Program. Until my class came along, very few students had washed out in this phase. That was unfortunate for us because some bean counter said the program was not paying for itself. He said more pilots should be washing out for it to be cost effective. I think we lost about ten men in the T-41.

They were being eliminated for the most minor things. One guy cut a corner taxiing in one day and got one wheel on the grass a little bit. He was washed back to another class. Everyone held his breath until we got out of there.

We were given an Orientation Briefing, and then we were introduced to our Instructors. Mine was Bill Fleming, and though he looked to be about thirty years old, I got the impression that he was one of the more experienced instructors in that program. Most of the other ones were about the same age as us. I wondered how they felt watching student after student moving on up to jets while they remained there doing the same thing over and over?

I got a surprise that morning. The School Manager asked for a show of hands of those who had gone through the Flight Indoctrination Program (FIP) while they were in ROTC. About two-thirds of my classmates raised their hands. He said, "Since you already have your Private Licenses, you men will get twelve hours of instruction and a final check ride. Those of you who did not go through FIP will get thirty hours." I kind of chuckled to myself. I didn't get to take FIP because I already had a Commercial Pilots License, and I would have to take extra hours because I didn't go through the FIP program. I didn't mind. I knew all of us would have to stay there until everyone finished, and I much preferred flying to sitting around.

Instructor Pilot Bill Fleming

Our first flight was called our "Dollar Ride", which meant it was kind of a freebie introduction to the airplane. There was no pressure involved and nothing was expected of the student. Bill gave me a briefing and then we went out to the airplane.

He had me follow through with my checklist as he did the preflight inspection on the airplane. He put me in the left seat and showed me how to adjust it. He warned, "Make sure the pin is securely in the hole Mike. If it's not, this seat could slide back on takeoff. That would not be good." I knew that because it happened to me one time. I didn't say anything.

We taxied out, and Bill said he would demonstrate the first takeoff. After takeoff he said, "We are just going out to the practice area and fly around a little bit. I will demonstrate some of the things we will be doing, but mostly I want you to get a feel for how this thing flies." I nodded.

We departed the pattern and climbed to twenty-five hundred feet. Bill rolled the wings left and right. He said, "This is the aileron control. It makes the airplane roll." Then he moved the rudder pedals left and right.

"These are the rudders. They control the yaw of the airplane."

He moved the yoke fore and aft. "This is the elevator, which changes the pitch attitude of the airplane." I said I understood.

"Okay then, you have the airplane. Just try to keep it straight and level." He made a mark on the windshield with a grease pencil and said, "That's the horizon. If you keep that mark lined up with the horizon you will stay level. That applies to turns too."

I flew the plane straight and level for a few minutes.

"That's fine Mike. Now make a gentle turn to the left."

I made the turn, using thirty degrees of bank and held my altitude without so much as a bobble.

"Try one to the right."

I did, with the same result. We did climbs, descents, turns in climbs, and turns in descents. I was concentrating hard and trying to do everything he said, as smoothly and perfectly as possible. After a while, Bill sat back in his seat and said, "All right Mike, it's time for you to fess up. How much flying time do you have?"

I said, "Mr. Fleming, I didn't want to mention this at all, but because you asked, I have to tell you. I hope you will keep this between just you and me because I don't want my classmates to know. I didn't go through FIP in college because I already had a Commercial Pilot's License. I have six hundred hours of total time - four hundred of them in a Cessna 172!"

"I suspected as much!"

"Mr. Flemming, I was taught to fly at small flight school. My two instructors were very good pilots, but I may have developed some bad habits that need correcting. I just want to learn to do it the way the Air Force does it, and if that means re-learning everything, so be it. I will do whatever it takes to accomplish that."

"Well Mike, with that attitude and your background, I think we will do just fine. So far I haven't seen anything I would change. These next thirty hours are going to be a lot of fun for both of us. And please call me Bill." On the way back to the airport he said, "Do you want to make the landing?" I said I would appreciate that!

On the bus ride back to the base, my thoughts drifted back to my first day at Ole Miss. I was so filled with doubts that day. I had no idea how I stacked up against the other athletes on that team. My confidence level was shaky but my hopes were high. Here at UPT it was different. I had spent the past eight years preparing for this. I was as ready for it as anyone could be. I knew I was a good pilot, and I was confident I would do very well in this program.

We had now reached the end of our first week in UPT. I told Jim I wanted to go out to the Officer's Club that night and see what it was like there on the weekend. He came too. We were having a few drinks with some of our classmates when I said I wanted to call home and talk to the folks. Jim was from a military family, so he knew a lot about life on base.

"Mike, there is a system called a MARS phone that we can use. Long distance is free on that phone. There is one at the Visiting Officer's Quarters next door. I've used it. Let's go over there."

When we got there, several other guys were in line to use

the phone. We had to wait our turn, so we started playing pool.

Colonel Chester J. Butcher

A few minutes later, a highly decorated, high-ranking officer walked in wearing his mess dress uniform with the name Butcher on the nametag. I had read in the base newspaper that Colonel Chester J. Butcher had been selected as the new Wing Commander at Webb Air Force Base. The article mentioned that Colonel Butcher had flown P-51 Mustangs in World War II. It listed all his other accomplishments in his distinguished career.

I had just enough alcohol in my system to quash any inhibitions I may have had, and I brazenly walked up to him and said, "Excuse me, Sir, you are Colonel Butcher aren't you?"

"Yes I am," he said, smiling.

Sticking out my hand, I said, "Sir, I'm Lieutenant Mike Trahan from Class 67C, and I read about you in the base newspaper. I just wanted to tell you that we are damn proud to have a fighter pilot like you for our new Wing Commander!"

He laughed, "Nice to meet you Mike." He recognized my Cajun name, and he asked me if I was from Louisiana. I told him I was ninety-nine percent Cajun, but that I was born in Orange, Texas. Jim introduced himself, and then Colonel Butcher was gone.

Jim looked at me, shaking his head, "You are one crazy hombre!" I wondered if I had just screwed up big time!

A couple of weeks later I got my answer to that question. I hadn't screwed up, and he was not offended by what I did. Chester Butcher was from Lafayette, and he was a true Cajun. He was also a "people person" and he got a big kick out of this brazen, half drunk, Cajun Student Pilot coming right up to him like I did.

I had been in the Stag Bar that night, and I decided to go into the main room of the club for dinner. I was wearing civilian clothes with no nametag to identify me. I saw Colonel Butcher talking with a bunch of other Colonels and their wives. I tried to sneak by them unnoticed and thought I had succeeded.

"Lieutenant Trahan, come over here. I want you to meet someone."

He had recognized and remembered me from that one brief encounter at the Visiting Officer Quarters. I walked over there amongst all those Senior Officers and their wives, feeling quite self-conscious. Colonel Butcher's smile put me at ease right away. He turned to his wife and said, "Harriet, this is Lieutenant Mike Trahan from 67C. He was the first person to welcome me to Webb Air Force Base! Mike is from

Orange, Texas."

He then proceeded to introduce me to every member of his Wing Staff and their wives. I thought, *Well, so much for going quietly through this program. Now everybody who runs everything on this base knows me by name.* But, I was also blown away that this World War II Hero and the Top Man at Webb Air Force Base remembered so much about me. That was the moment my lifelong admiration for Chester J. Butcher was born.

The T-41 Program couldn't go by fast enough for us. We just wanted it done, so we could start flying real Air Force airplanes. We wanted to get into those jets!

Getting through this phase was a breeze for me. Every time Bill introduced a new maneuver, it was one that I had already practiced dozens of times back home.

"Mike, I have never seen anyone master new things as quickly as you do!"

I said, "Bill, I think it's time for me to finish my confession to you. A friend of mine who is in G Class sent me the T-41 Maneuvers Manual a while back. I've been practicing all this stuff for six months!"

He laughed. "Well, that explains that!"

I soloed on my ninth ride in the T-41. Right after my first solo takeoff the right door popped open. It only opened an inch or two, so nobody could see it on the ground. This had happened to me on the 172 I flew back in Orange, so I knew what to do. I waited until I turned so that side of the airplane was not visible to the tower. Then I opened the window on that door. I knew I had to do that to equalize the pressure on both sides of the door in order to get it closed. Once it was closed I closed the window and continued on with my sortie.

If I had reported the open door I might have been given a failing grade on my solo for not following the checklist and ensuring that the door was closed and locked. The way things were going in that program that could have led to my being eliminated from the program. So, I didn't say anything about it. The rest of the ride went well. I got an excellent on my landings from the Instructor Pilot in the tower.

At my fifteenth hour I took my Mid-Phase Check Ride with a guy named Lewis. My raw score was 83%, but when they factored in the standard score it bumped up to 93%

At the thirty hours point I took my Final Check Ride with Lewis again. This time my raw score was 90% for a standard score of 96.6%. I also made 100% on the T-41 program written exam. My cumulative average for all three scores was 96%. At the end of the T-41 Program I was ranked #1 in the Class. I was off to a great start!

Jim and I got a call the next day. Our BOQ apartment was ready for move in, and we moved in that same day. Once we got on Base, we both felt we were finally in the Air Force instead of on the outside looking in. It felt good.

We had an upstairs apartment on the northwest corner of one of the buildings. The apartment consisted of two bedrooms, a bathroom, and a living room. Each bedroom had a single bed, a desk, a chair and a lamp. There was a closet, which was adequate for our civilian and military clothes. It was fairly Spartan but comfortable enough.

We shared a stair landing with another apartment. That apartment was a mirror image of ours. Our neighbors were Air Force Academy Graduate, Allen Natella, and Phil Holdiness.

Allen had broken his ankle in a parasailing accident, and right before we went into T-37's he washed back from B Class to our class. He was disappointed about that, but it was better than washing out. Jim and I became good friends with both Allen and Phil.

Our daily Flying/Academic schedule worked in a way that if we flew in the morning, we would report for duty at 0600, and our flying period ended at noon. We took a break for lunch and at 1300 hours we would go to Academics. If we had Academics first, we reported for class at 0750. Flying started at 1300 hours. The two sections of the class alternated morning and evening flying. We changed over every other week.

It didn't take long for our academic load to increase. Our classes were always a step ahead of our flying. For example, we had been in T-41's just a week when we started taking courses relating to the T-37. We took T-37 Engineering, High Speed Aerodynamics, T-37 Normal and Emergency Procedures, etc. We also took a course in High Altitude Physiology where we learned about hypoxia and hyperventilation. Part of our Physiology course included a trip to the Altitude Chamber.

The Altitude Chamber was very interesting. We were all fitted with oxygen masks and were breathing 100% oxygen. An enlisted man was in there with us. He told us we would experience the equivalent of a sudden loss of pressurization and the chamber would almost immediately assume an internal altitude of 25,000 feet. He said when we got up there we would experience some abdominal cramps. The gases trapped inside our bodies caused this cramping.

"It is perfectly acceptable to pass gas in the chamber. In

fact, if you don't fart you are in for some pretty bad pain."

Suddenly, there was a loud noise and I noticed the altimeter in the chamber climbing rapidly. In about thirty seconds it indicated 25,000 feet. Everything felt pretty much the same to me except my stomach. When I looked down I saw that it was starting to distend. I got a sudden urge to fart, and I let one rip. So did everyone else in there.

"Okay, men, now that we have the atmosphere completely polluted in here, it's time to take off the masks. Pick a partner. One of you will remove his mask and the other guy will stay on oxygen and watch his partner carefully." God that place stank!

We did some exercises and discovered that it didn't take long to become incapacitated by hypoxia. We were told to remember every symptom we had before we lost useful consciousness. That would help us recognize them if we ever encountered hypoxia in flight. It was a valuable lesson.

The next day we were back at the physiology building for some more training. This time we would get to ride the Ejection Seat Trainer. It was pretty realistic. We strapped in, just like we would in the airplane, and when given the signal, we raised the ejection handles and shot about thirty feet up a rail. It was a pretty exciting ride. It made me almost want to try it for real some day.

It made sense to get parachute training right after ejection seat training. If we were successful in getting out of the jet and away from the ejection seat, we still had a ways to go before we were safe. Our parachute had to open so we could float down to the ground. To simulate this, we were hung in parachute harness to see what that felt like. We called it "Suspended Agony." The first two classes got to do some parasailing to experience a descent in a chute, but the program was suspended because too many people were getting hurt. Allen Natella's parasailing accident was the final straw.

The biggest hazard in parachuting was the landing. We were taught the proper way to make a Parachute Landing Fall, or PLF. We jumped from five feet up into a sand pit to practice this. We learned what to do if we were landing in water, in trees, into power lines The last phase of parachute training was releasing the chute, so it would not drag us in a high wind or drown us in the water.

I was sitting in my living room listening to records on my stereo when Natella walked in. He was wearing his flight helmet with the oxygen mask and hose hanging free.

"My buddies in 67B tell me it is helpful to wear your helmet and mask to get used to them before you go flying. It keeps you from feeling so claustrophobic the first time you put them on in the airplane." He buckled his mask over his face.

I went to my room and got my helmet and mask and did the same thing. When Jim Roberts walked in, he started laughing and said, "What the hell are you two doing?" We told him and he went to his room and got his helmet and mask too.

There we sat, three would-be jet pilots breathing through a little rubber hose and listening to The Holly Ridge Strings playing the Four Season's greatest hits. Oh, how I wish someone had taken a picture of that.

Chapter 3

The T-37 Program

T-37 "Tweety Bird"

The big day had arrived. Class 67C had finally made it to jet training. Our first Air Force Jet was the T-37 *Tweety Bird* aka *Tweet* aka *The Six Thousand Pound Dog Whistle*. It was named all those things because when its engines were at idle, they produced an excruciating very high pitch whining sound. The sound was so bad that if you were anywhere near it without ear protection, it would cause immediate damage to your hearing. Consequently, we never stepped out of our line shack without our heavy-duty earmuffs on.

The Tweet, a straight winged, sub-sonic trainer built by the Cessna Aircraft Corporation, was a twin engine, two-place airplane where the pilots sat side by side. I found it a little ironic that I had come this far, and all I had flown in the Air Force were Cessnas! I had started out in Cessnas eight years ago, and I was still flying Cessnas!

Each section of the class had its own line shack and its own set of Instructor Pilots. The line shack was a long, narrow building that contained a couple of offices, a bathroom, an equipment room where we stored our helmets, parachutes, and other flight gear, and a large briefing room. Our section was down to twenty-four students, and there were eight Instructor Pilots (IPs) there to teach us. Each IP had three students. I got very lucky and drew Lt. William A. "Bill" Zamboni for my instructor. Joining me at Zamboni's table were Boyce Core and John King.

John King, Bill Zamboni, Mike

Bill actually started out in the Nevada Air Guard where he flew B-57 and F-86 aircraft and had only recently come on active duty with the regular Air Force. He was an excellent pilot and a great instructor, very low key and quite cool in the airplane. Nothing seemed to bother him. I liked him right away.

Captain Gene Taft was our flight commander. Gene was a great leader for us. His tall, thin, and distinguished looking appearance gave me the impression he would be easy to get along with, but it would be best not to cross him.

When it was time for my "Dollar Ride" in the T-37, Zamboni gave me a thorough pre-flight briefing, and we donned our parachutes and ear protection and headed out to the ramp. The noise from the T-37's starting up was almost excruciating. The noise was coupled with a strong odor of J-P4 jet fuel and jet exhaust in the air. I knew, the first time I experienced those things, I would never forget them, and I haven't. I can hear and smell them to this day.

When we got to the airplane, Bill showed me how to check the Air Force Form 781, the aircraft maintenance log. If there were any issues with the airplane, they would be listed. All issues must be cleared and an Airworthiness Release signed before we could go any further. Everything was in order, so we signed our names in the book and continued with the pre-flight walk around inspection. The aircraft check list covered every item from walk around to shut down. Bill took me through this one and I followed up using my checklist.

Before I stepped into the airplane, Bill gave me a thorough briefing on the ejection seat. He showed me where the safety pin should be – it was there. He said we never removed that pin until we were seated and ready to go. This was to prevent accidental firing of the seat.

After we strapped in and plugged in we went through cockpit orientation. We used hot-mike interphone connections between the IP and the student. That meant we could hear everything the other pilot said at all times. We could even hear each other's breathing! I became so self-conscious of my breathing I caught myself holding my breath half the time. Bill saw what I was doing and laughed.

"You will get used to that, so don't worry about it. But whatever you do, don't hold your breath. I don't want you passing out on me!"

I remembered how much trouble I had picking out the pilot's voice over all the other voices when I rode in the T-37 at Summer Training. Now it was better. I was already used to Bill's voice, and I noticed when he transmitted outside of the airplane, the tone was different. Before engine start, Bill told me to strap on my oxygen mask. We didn't want to breathe in any more exhaust fumes before flying.

After engine start, Bill and I took a salute from our Aircraft Crew Chief, and he called Webb Tower for taxi clearance. It was pretty chilly that day, so Bill closed the canopy as soon as we started rolling. We taxied along the west side of the huge ramp past rows of T-37's and T-38's. We were taking off to the south that day, so when we got to Runway 18L, we stopped and waited for crossing clearance. The T-38's used the inside runway (18L / 36R), and the Tweets used the outside runway (18R / 36L). Bill had already switched to the Mobil Runway Supervisory Unit (Mobil RSU) and we soon were cleared to cross.

There was an RSU at the approach end of each of the runways manned by two instructors. One controlled the T-38 Runway and the other controlled the T-37 Runway. Each RSU had a name. Ours was Peckerwood! Each IP and student had his own call sign. Zamboni was Snappy, and I was Snappy 8.

As we approached Runway 18R, Peckerwood said, "Snappy, you are cleared for takeoff!" Zamboni answered, "Snappy cleared for takeoff. Canopy down and locked. Light out!" Bill lined us up in the center of the runway and advanced the throttles to the stop. Power management in jets was so much easier than it was in prop airplanes. To go all you had to do was push the throttle forward and to slow you just pulled it back. There were no propeller pitch controls to fool with, and at least in fighter and trainer jets, we didn't have to worry about over-boosting the engines.

The Tweet slowly accelerated at first, and then it started picking up speed rapidly. We were airborne quicker than I thought we would be. I was mostly impressed with how smooth it felt. There was no vibration at all. We climbed out of the traffic pattern and flew out to our designated area.

The practice areas were cut into pies in the sky. We worked off radials from the Webb VOR/TACAN navigation beacon. By using radials and distance we could carve out a pie-shaped piece of sky that was all ours. No other airplanes *should* be in that airspace while we had it. When we were clear of the traffic pattern Bill called Fort Worth Center for clearance into our area. We were cleared in immediately.

We climbed to Flight Level 200 and just drove around in the sky a little while. This lesson was very similar to my first ride in the T-41, grease pencil and all. Bill gave me control of the airplane, and I just loved the way it felt. It was very responsive to the controls, and it actually flew like a high performance light twin. We flew around for an hour, and Bill took us in for the landing. The Tweet looked fairly easy to land, and it was. I now had my first hour of jet time in my logbook.

As we were taxiing in, Bill said, "Good ride, Trahan. How do you feel?" I told him I felt great, but I had felt a little claustrophobic for the first fifteen minutes and that hearing our breathing was distracting, but I got over it pretty quickly.

"Well, you looked very relaxed, especially since this was your first jet ride. I think you will do just fine. The first phase of your training will be Contact Flying. We will concentrate on maneuvers, takeoffs, and landings."

"That works for me Sir!" .

Air Force flight suits (coveralls) were cool looking. The suit itself was a dull greenish color, but all of them were festooned with colorful patches that made them look pretty sharp. These patches identified the pilot and the organizations he was attached to. For example, on the left chest area we wore our nametag and a set of wings if we were rated pilots. Students just had a name strip. On the right chest area we wore the STURON (Student Squadron) Patch. On our right arm was the 3561st Section patch. On the left arm the IP's wore a patch depicting the aircraft they flew – either the T-37 or the T-38. Each student wore his Class Patch on his left shoulder. Each Class had the privilege of picking the theme of their patch.

Our World Famous Class Patch

Class 67C chose to use Charlie Schultz's Snoopy, the World War One Flying Ace, on our patch. First Lieutenant John Molis, of the 60th Section, came up with the idea. John and Paul Baker drew it up. The patch was about three inches in diameter, and it depicted Snoopy flying his doghouse with his leather helmet and his scarf flying in the breeze. It was perfect! Our class motto was "Curse You Red Baron!" That motto wound up being tagged on a railroad overpass in downtown Big Spring sometime during that year.

Since ours was the first UPT class to use Snoopy, we thought it might wise to contact Charles Schultz and get permission to use his copyrighted character. He wrote back and gave us his enthusiastic approval.

Something clicked in our class when we put that patch on. Everyone on the base loved it, because it was unique, cheerful, and funny. The base newspaper did a feature story on it, and that story was picked up and published by "The Air Force Times". We were world famous! People couldn't help but look at it and grin when we passed by. We wore it with great pride! I think that is when the Spirit of Snoopy Flight was born.

As I mentioned before, Allen Natella had washed back into our Class from B Class because he broke his ankle. He was getting well, but he was still DNIF (Duty Not Involving Flying). Our class had been in the T-37's for a couple of weeks, and we had just finished flying the morning schedule. We all went to the Officer's Club for lunch. We were still in our snazzy-looking flight suits.

When I got to the head of the buffet line, I noticed Allen standing there. There was a very beautiful girl standing by his side. She was fairly tall, about 5' 8" and trim. She had short auburn hair and a great smile! Natella was introducing her to each of his classmates as we filed by. The closer I got to her, the better she looked. When I was about five feet from her, I got my first good look at her eyes! They were the most beautiful eyes I had ever seen!

When it was my turn, Allen said, "Sheila, I would like to introduce you to Mike Trahan. Mike, this is Sheila Niedzwiecki!" I said, "How do you do Sheila. It's nice to meet you." She said, "Nice to meet you too Mike." And then I said, "Would you answer a question for me?" She said, "Sure, what is your question?" I said, "How do you spell your last name?" She had a puzzled look on her face and said, "Now, why do you want to know that?" I replied, "Because it will help me pronounce it and remember it." She seemed pleased with my answer. She smiled and said, "It's N-I-E-D-Z-W-I-E-C-K-I." I replied, "Okay Sheila, thank you. I think I've got it now!" She smiled again, and then it was time for me to move along. As I walked away a thought crossed my mind.

Allen Natella is one lucky guy. I hope I find a girl like her some day.

Allen later told me that Sheila was a Stewardess for Braniff International Airline, based in Dallas. He met her by accident one night when he was pulling Officer of The Day duty. She called the base trying to find one of the students there. Allen said he couldn't find the guy, but they became engaged in a long conversation. She told him if he was ever in Dallas to look her up, and she gave him her number. He was there the next weekend.

Two weeks later Sheila was in Big Spring visiting Allen again. I was standing on the stair landing of our BOQ, watching the sunset, when she walked by.

"Hi, Mike!"

"Hi, Sheila, how are you?"

"I'm fine, thanks."

She got a playful grin on her face and said, "By the way, can you spell my last name for me?"

"N-I-E-D-Z-W-I-E-C-K-I, and it's pronounced Niedzwiecki!"

She smiled. "Good!" Then she went into Allen's apartment.

Sheila came to visit Allen several times over the next few months. The more I got to know her, the more I enjoyed being around her. She was very relaxed and easy to talk to.

Sheila Niedzwiecki

If someone were to ask me to characterize my first ten hours in the T-37, I could answer with just one word – FUN! Contact flying was all about getting to know the airplane and its performance ranges, from stalls to maximum airspeed. Like Clarence and Ed Feuge before him, Bill Zamboni stressed getting everything you could get out of an airplane. That meant flying it to the very edges of its performance envelope.

For example, the standard entry speed for a loop in the Tweet was 310 knots. Bill had me do the first one at 310 knots and then enter each successive loop ten knots slower than the last one. He made me do that until the airplane could not make it around a loop.

"Now you know how slowly you can go and still loop this airplane!"

He then added, "Trahan, this may come in handy some day if you have someone following you around in a loop and you don't want him back there." When we were inverted at the top of the loop, Bill reached out and extended the landing gear! That extra drag made the second half of that loop a lot smaller than the first half. If someone had been chasing me, he would have overshot, and I would have been on his tail.

Cockpit shot in the T-37

Bill made sure I was very proficient in recovering from unusual attitudes, especially vertical and inverted recoveries. One time he showed me a maneuver that was fun, but it was not in the syllabus. He pointed us straight at the sky and said, "We are going to hold this attitude until it quits flying. I will freeze the elevator so it doesn't overstress if we slide backward. Most likely it will break either backward or forward." We kept going up and up, and then the airplane stopped climbing and started sliding backward. Then the nose snapped over the top and we were in a vertical dive. It was an exciting maneuver to ride through, but there were many more fun maneuvers to come.

We did slow flight, aileron rolls, barrel rolls, loops, Cuban eights, Split S, Immelmans, slow flight, high speed dives, the complete stall series, and of course, the dreaded spin series.

Not many of my classmates had ever seen a spin. The syllabus in the Flight Indoctrination Program didn't call for them, nor did the T-41 program. In fact, not many civilian schools taught spins any more. I was fortunate because the Feuge brothers were old school. They felt that any pilot should know how to get out of a spin if he ever got into one, and they taught them to me. Spins were exciting in a Champ, but in the T-37 they were beyond exciting. That thing would spin like a top.

We climbed up to twenty-three thousand feet for our spin entries. Bill said if we hadn't recovered by ten thousand, we had to bail out. We were usually straight and level by fifteen thousand. He had me do three or four revolutions before initiating recovery. Then he said, "Now, I want to show you what will happen if you release a little back pressure on the stick during a spin. I will demonstrate one for you." We were supposed to keep the stick full aft until we initiated the recovery.

We climbed back to FL 230 and entered a normal spin. After a couple of turns, Bill released a little backpressure and held the stick there. The rotation rate doubled immediately. The view outside the windscreen was just a blur. I know my breathing rate doubled too. This one was new to me. Bill remained calm and composed and he said, "Okay, recovery is the same. Opposite rudder, wait one turn, stick forward, rudders neutral and recover from the dive." The recovery worked just fine. We lived to fly another day, and my breathing returned to normal.

One day Bill was showing me a high-speed dive, and all of a sudden there was a loud popping sound and then a great rush of wind noise. I nearly jumped out of my seat, but Bill just sat over there like nothing had happened. I said, "Lieutenant, what the hell is that?" He pointed up to the canopy and said, "The canopy has popped due to the reduced pressure over it, and it's being held on by the canopy locks."

I looked up, and I could see the locks, but I could also see about an inch of space between the canopy and the windshield frame. As soon as we slowed down, the canopy went back into place. I looked over at him and said, "Thanks for the warning!" He laughed and said, "I look forward to this with every student. You all react the same way. It scares the shit out of you!"

On another flight we were flying along and I felt the stick moving back into my hand. I was not touching the trim button, but my Instructor was. He was trying to simulate runaway trim so I would have to demonstrate the recovery procedure. Instead, I just froze the stick in place with opposing pressure. The load was getting a little heavy, but I was not about to let that nose wobble.

Bill started looking around the cockpit trying to figure out why the airplane wasn't climbing. It wasn't climbing because I wouldn't let it climb. In exasperation he said, "I've got the airplane!"

"Roger, Sir, you've got it!"

I let go, and as soon as I released the stick, it slammed

back into his hand, and the airplane lurched skyward. He re-covered the aircraft and said, in a disgusted voice, "You damn gorilla!"

I was laughing so hard I almost missed his comment.

I can say this about Bill Zamboni. I could not have had a better person teaching me how to fly a jet. In the first place, he was a lot of fun to fly with. But, he also knew his stuff, and he knew how to impart the additional techniques he learned while flying F-86's. I think he was grooming me to be a fighter pilot. Zamboni was my IP for every pre-solo flight ex-cept two.

After five or six rides in the area practicing flight maneu-vers, it was time to start doing some pattern work. We al-ways got two or three landings at the end of each mission, but now we were spending the entire flight on takeoffs and landings. The Tweet was relatively easy to land. However, getting used to the Air Force's three hundred sixty degree overhead landing pattern was something else.

The pattern worked like this: We flew over the runway at pattern altitude, and when we reached mid-field, we did what was called a Pitch Out. That was a sixty-degree banked turn of one hundred eighty degrees. That put us on down-wind. We lowered the flaps and put out the landing gear and maintained altitude while slowing to approach speed. When the end of the runway was forty-five degrees behind us, we reduced power and started a continuous one hundred eighty degree descending turn to final. The goal was to be lined up with the runway at one mile out and three hundred feet above ground level. A perfect pattern would be an uninter-rupted descent from the time we reduced power to touch-down. That took some practice, but after a few tries I had it down.

Right before my solo flight, Captain Gene Taft, our Flight Commander, flew with me. For some reason I was nervous with him. I shouldn't have been. He was an easy-going guy. I believe Captain Taft flew with every student in the section at one time or another. I didn't know that at the time though. I thought I was getting some kind of no-notice check ride.

I was doing my cockpit preflight checklist, and every time I accomplished an item, I would tug at my flight gloves to make sure they were snug. After about the tenth time I did that, he said, "What's wrong with your gloves, Trahan?"

"Nothing Sir!"

"Well, stop tugging at them then. That's just a nervous tick!"

After that I just relaxed and had a good ride with him.

Chapter 4

Christmas Break

I had had only five rides in the T-37 when it was time for Christmas Break. We were given two weeks free of duty, and, if we wanted to, we could go home. To be honest, I didn't want to go home. I wanted to stay there and fly the jet.

However, when I walked through the door at home, Dad gave me the warmest greeting he had ever given me. Of course, Mom was in the kitchen, putting the finishing touches on a big pot of shrimp gumbo. She was glad to see me too.

At dinner I could not stop talking about flight school, and they wanted to know all about it. Christmas was nice. I visited some friends during my time off, but mostly I stayed around the house. My time at home was brief, but I was more than ready to go back to Webb. I had a jet to solo!

On 12 January, it was time for Snoopy Flight to solo the jet. A group of us were told to report to the flight line an hour earlier. We were going to be bused out to an Air Force Auxiliary Field, Copperhead, which was located about fifty miles east of Webb near Sweetwater, Texas. There was one runway and an RSU there. They also kept a staffed fire truck on hand. This was where we were going to make our first solos in the T-37. When we got there, there was only one Tweet on the field, and we wondered if we were going to have to take turns with that one airplane. Thirty minutes later the sky was filled with Tweets. Our classmates, who were not soloing that day, flew in with their instructors.

All the airplanes were refueled, and Zamboni and I walked out to one of them.

"Let's just stay in the traffic pattern and shoot landings."

After my third landing, he said, "Okay, Trahan, taxi over there next to the RSU. I'm ready to get out of this thing!" When we got to the designated spot, I parked the airplane and Bill told me to shut down the right engine.

"Just stay in the pattern and shoot landings until you are down to twenty minutes of fuel. Then make a full stop. Don't make me look bad by busting your ass out there!"

He secured his ejection seat with the safety pin, opened the canopy, and stepped out. When he was safely away from the airplane, he gave me the signal to start the right engine. Once the engine was started, the Crew Chief gave me a salute, and I saluted back. Then I looked over at Bill. He gave me a salute, too, with his middle finger! I returned his salute in kind. I closed my canopy, ran the before takeoff checklist and called Copperhead Control for taxi instructions. Captain Taft was manning Copperhead that day.

As I approached the end of the runway, I heard the words, "Snappy 8, you are cleared for takeoff!"

I taxied smartly onto the runway, lined up with the centerline, and without hesitation, advanced both throttles to the stop. The Tweet seemed to have a little more pep on that takeoff. I'm sure some of it was my imagination, but also the reduction in weight probably contributed, and it was also a cold day. Whatever the reason, that little airplane leaped into the sky like a homesick angel. As I climbed to pattern altitude, I felt complete exhilaration. Exactly eight years and four days after my first solo in the Champ, I was having a "Second First Solo" in an *Air Force jet!*

On my first downwind leg, I noticed I was drifting toward the runway, so I put in a little left crab angle to maintain spacing, and I made a mental note to make a steeper turn to base and final to keep from overshooting the runway. Apparently, there was a pretty strong crosswind at pattern altitude, and it was coming from the east. It wasn't there when Bill and I were shooting landings.

During my first approach I noticed that once I was out of five hundred feet the wind calmed down. Lining up with the runway on final was not a problem because I had compensated for the crosswind in advance. It was not so for the guy behind me!

George D'Angelo was also soloing that day, and he was having trouble getting on the ground. He kept overshooting final, and Captain Taft kept sending him around. After George's second go-around, I keyed my microphone and said, "Captain Taft, there is a strong crosswind out of the east at pattern altitude. It goes away at five hundred feet." I hoped that information would help him talk D'Angelo down.

"Roger the crosswind, Snappy 8. See me in my office when we get back to Base."

"Oh crap, what have I done wrong now?"

Taft told George to widen out his pattern, and that should keep him from overshooting on final. George did what he Taft told him and made three successful landings. After we were parked on the ramp, I walked over to George and congratulated him on is solo. He congratulated me back. I didn't say anything else, and neither did he.

I worried all the way back to Big Spring. I really thought I was in some kind of big trouble. Captain Taft was already in his office when we got back to the line shack. Bill went in to see him first, and when he came back, he said, "Trahan, the Flight Commander is waiting to see you!"

I walked into Capt. Taft's office, snapped him a salute, and said, "Lt Trahan reporting as ordered, Sir." He said, "Lt. Trahan, have a seat." And then he started chewing my ass.

"Trahan, NEVER use names over the radio. There is a good reason for that. We don't want to give anyone who might be listening any more information than necessary. The proper call sign for that RSU is Copperhead. You need to brush up on your radio discipline. Is that understood?"

"Yes, Sir, loud and clear," I responded sheepishly.

I was about to leave his office, feeling like shit, when he stood up, walked over to me, and smiled. He shook my hand and said, "Congratulations Mike, you did an excellent job out there today!" I felt better immediately, but I was still a little weak in the knees when I walked out of there.

When I got back to Zamboni's table, Darol Holsman was making his speech. It was tradition for the solo pilot to make as grandiose a speech as possible. Nobody told me that that, but it wouldn't have mattered anyway. I was so drained from all the day's activities I just didn't have much energy left in me. Consequently, my speech came out flat and devoid of emotion. Zamboni stopped me.

"No, no, no. That won't do! Try that again, and let's have a little enthusiasm this time!"

So, I started again.

"You men witnessed something today that you will all tell your grandkids about! You just saw the Greatest Aviator of All Time making his first solo in a jet airplane. Never, in its storied history, has a T-37 been flown with more precision, skill, and just plain pizazz than that one was flown with today! Sonnets

will be written, songs will be sung, and legends will abound about what took place at Copperhead this morning. This was an aviation feat that will never be equaled." I embellished it even more as I went along. By the time I finished, everyone in the room was laughing.

It was also tradition for the student to buy his instructor a bottle of booze after his first solo. When Zamboni told us that the week before, he added, "I like Beefeater Gin!"

After I sat down, I reached into my briefcase and pulled out a paper bag. Inside was a pint of Thunderbird Wine – the cheapest booze money could buy. There was also a note - *"To Lieutenant Bill Zamboni, in appreciation for his flight instruction and in recognition of the quality of that instruction."* I handed it to him under the table. When he looked and saw the Thunderbird, he frowned and said, "Screw you Trahan!" He pouted the rest of the period. I think he was genuinely pissed off at me.

When it came time to go home, I waited until Bill left. Then I snuck outside and watched, from behind the corner of the line shack, as he opened his car door. On the front seat was another brown paper bag. On this one I had written, "Thank you, Bill!" Inside was an Imperial Quart of Beefeater Gin! He shook his head, as if to say, "That turd got to me again." And then, he looked up at the sky and smiled.

T-37 Solo Certificate

Sheila Niedzwiecki and Allen Natella had become an "item." She was in Big Spring just about every other week-end. Allen and I had become good friends, so naturally I spent time with them at the club and during our Class get-togethers. As a result, she and I were developing a nice comfortable friendship, too.

One day I said, "Hey Sheila, why don't you fix me up with a sexy stewardess like you?"

"I've been thinking about that, Mike, and I believe I have the perfect girl for you. Her name is Donna, and she is a good Catholic girl and a school teacher."

"No, no, you misunderstand my needs. I need a sexy stewardess – like you!"

She laughed and said, "You will like Donna!"

Two weeks later Donna came out to Big Spring with Sheila. We had a nice time, and I did like her. She was a very nice, attractive woman, and she was very sweet. We hit it off right away! A couple of weekends after that, Allen and I drove to Dallas to visit Sheila and Donna. We had a great weekend with them, and when we left late on Sunday evening, there was a promise of more visits to come. We got back to the base after midnight. We were scheduled for the early flight period the next morning.

When I got to the line shack, the first thing I did was check the flight schedule. I was hoping I would not be flying that day because I was tired, and I didn't feel that well. Unfortunately, mine was the first solo flight on the schedule. I donned my flight gear and dragged my butt to the airplane.

This was supposed to be an area flight for practicing maneuvers, and I attempted to do that. But, I was graying out at just three G's. Even 100% oxygen didn't help. I flew straight and level and just looked around the area. I was getting sleepy just boring holes in the sky, so I decided to go back to Webb and shoot some landings. I thought the action and excitement of the traffic pattern would take my mind off how I felt.

When I got to pattern altitude, I hit some rough choppy air. I was on outside initial approach and still some distance from the field. I felt like I was going to throw up, and I started seeing spots in front of my eyes. Suddenly, one of those spots became an airplane! It was entering inside initial from the right, and we were very close to each other. I slammed the throttles to the stop and pulled back on the stick to avoid hitting him. The next thing I knew I was going straight up and running out of airspeed and ideas. I realized I'd better do something quick and do it right, or I would bust my ass. I executed a vertical recovery! It was a good thing Bill had taught me how to nurse that airplane through low speed unusual attitudes. I was very close to stalling out and spinning in.

I came back around, re-entered initial, and requested a full stop landing. When I got to the line shack, Zamboni said, "You don't look so good!" I told him I thought I might be coming down with the flu. He said, "Go home and go to bed. Give me a call this evening and let me know how you are."

That night I got a call from Glen Doss. He and I spoke on the phone just about every other day. I asked him if he had flown that day, and he said, "Yes, I did, and I saw the craziest thing. I was on initial and something out of the ordinary caught my eye. It was in the T-37 pattern. I looked over there and saw a Tweet going straight up! I guess that guy recovered, because I didn't see any fire trucks on my next pattern."

"So what did you do today Mike?"

One day I was at the airplane getting ready for another solo flight. I was signing the Form 781 when I heard this voice behind me say, "How ya doin', Mike?" in a strong Cajun accent. I turned around and discovered the voice came from my cousin Lynward Oubre, from Loreauville, Louisiana. Lynward was the crew chief on that airplane that day. We had a nice family reunion right there on the ramp. I asked him how long he had been at Webb and he said just a few weeks. He said my mother told him I was at Webb and to look for me. I pointed at the airplane and said, "Did you check it good?"

He laughed. "Hell, for you, Cousin, I'll check it twice!" We both did the walk around and continued our visit.

After takeoff, I noticed a warning light on the instrument panel. It was a failed fuel boost pump indication. I called Peckerwood RSU and said, "Snappy 8 requesting closed pattern. I've got a failed boost pump indication." The controller said to check the switch, but I guess I clanked up because I couldn't see it. I just wanted to get that airplane on the ground. The Dash One (Flight Manual) says that, if you get negative G forces with a failed boost pump, the engines could flame out.

When I landed and ran my shut down checklist, I noticed the boost pump switch was already OFF! Lynward climbed on the wing and leaned into the cockpit to see what was wrong.

"Wazzamatter, Mike, you break my airplane?"

"No Len, I just screwed up and forgot to turn the boost pump on. Now I have to go inside and face the music."

I asked him to refuel the Tweet, and said I would probably be back to finish my mission.

"I'll top it off and have it ready for you."

When I got to the briefing room, I saw Captain Taft standing at Zamboni's table. When they saw me they both frowned.

"What are you doing in here?"

"Sir, I screwed up and forgot to turn the boost pump on. Then I made an emergency landing and came back to the ramp. When I realized what I had done, I didn't know what to do. Should I crank up again and go fly or should I come in here?"

"Get back out there and finish your mission Lieutenant!"

That was the only time I received a grade of "Fair" in the

T-37 program.

One day Bill took me up on an instrument ride. In order to simulate instrument conditions, we had a big visor that fit over our helmet. It blocked out everything but the instrument panel in front of us. It was pretty effective.

Bill was introducing me to one of the most basic of all instrument maneuvers – the Vertical S-A. The Vertical S-A started from level flight. Then you added power and climbed at a constant airspeed at a rate of five hundred feet per minute to five hundred feet above your initial altitude. When you reached your target altitude, you smoothly transitioned from a climb to a descent of five hundred feet per minute, back to your original altitude. It was a very boring maneuver.

I had not slept well the night before, and there I was, under that hood, where Bill could not see my eyes. I was so sleepy. I fought it as long as I could, but despite all my efforts, I drifted off to sleep. I heard this faint voice in my earphones, "and that is how you do the Vertical S A. You got that? Trahan, you got that?" He flipped the hood off my helmet and saw that my eyes were closed. He exclaimed, "Dammit! Are you asleep???" I jerked awake as Bill slammed the stick to the side and put us in a continuous, and very rapid, aileron roll. I lost track of how many revolutions we made.

He kept repeating, "Don't you ever fall asleep on me again!"

I believe he was truly mad at me.

Air Force pilots got some of their instrument training on the ground. In the old days they used an electronic trainer called a Link. The Link had all the necessary instruments, and even had some motion, but it didn't resemble any particular airplane. When I went through training, we had Flight Simulators that replicated the cockpits of a particular airplane right down to the smallest detail. At Webb we had both T-37 and T-38 Simulators. They were nothing like the old trainer but they were still affectionately called the Link.

The weather was too bad for flying that day, and when Bill showed up at the table I just knew someone was going to the Link with him. Apparently, he had a big weekend, and it showed. Frankly, he looked like hell. When he sat down, he said, "Trahan, get your gear. We're going to the Link!"

As soon as we were in the Simulator, Bill closed the canopy and leaned back in his seat. He was sound asleep before I finished my pre-start checklist. I flew around for an hour and a half and he never stirred!

It was during this flight that my diabolical plot was hatched. I wanted to get him back for waking me up on that Instrument Flight. When it was about time for us to go back to the Line Shack, I pushed the test button to light up both of the Engine Fire Handles and I yelled, "FIRE!! BAILOUT, BAILOUT, BAILOUT!"

Bill lurched awake and immediately reached for his ejection handles. He was about to pull the trigger when he realized that he had no helmet on, that he was not wearing a parachute, and that we were on the ground in the Simulator!

He just muttered to himself - "Dammit, Dammit, Dammit!"

I looked over at him and said, "Paybacks are hell aren't they?"

When it came time to find out how I was doing in the jet, I went up with Check Pilot Major Ethun for my Contact Mid-

Phase Check. I received a raw score of 77% for a standard score of 91%. Things were going very well for me, and my grades were holding up in academics as well.

I had chosen Webb AFB because of its good flying weather. However, the area was not without its hazards. For example, we could take off in perfectly clear weather and be enjoying a great flight when a weather recall for all Webb Aircraft would blast across the airways. When they transmitted a recall, you got to the base as soon as possible. The most likely reason for the clear day recall was a dust storm approaching the base, and most times we had very little advanced warning of approaching dust storms, which moved visibility from unlimited to practically zero-zero in a dust storm.

Another weather phenomenon at Webb was the Dust Devil. Though not related to dust storms or thunderstorms, Dust Devils had a mind of their own. They looked like small tornadoes made entirely of dust and seldom exceeded fifty feet in diameter. However, they could play havoc with an airplane that had slowed to landing speed and was three hundred feet above the ground. I saw a Tweet ahead of me encountering one of those little things and almost got flipped inverted. Fortunately, the pilot got it out of the dust devil before that happened, and he was able to recover and go around. By then, I had already started my go around.

West Texas is also known for huge thunderstorms that occasionally pop up. We usually had good warnings for those. Thunderstorm recalls were usually not as frantic as the dust storm recalls, but occasionally we had to race the weather in. Several times a year we would get a call at our line shack to go help the crew chiefs put hail guards on the wings of our airplanes. Hail guards were padded canvas en-velopes, which we slipped over the wing and secured to the fuselage. We also had a canopy cover which acted like in-flated parachutes if the wind caught them just right. Several of our classmates were banged up from being dragged across the ramp by a sudden gust of wind while trying to get the planes covered.

Birds, particularly Sandhill Cranes, could be a flight haz-ard. Sandhill Cranes are migratory birds about the size of a Snow Goose, weighing anywhere from three to six pounds.

One morning we set to go flying when word came down that a pilot from Reese AFB in Lubbock, Texas, had just been killed in a T-37. Two instructor pilots were flying the Weather Reconnaissance Aircraft when they encountered a flock of Sandhill Cranes. One of the cranes crashed through the windscreen and into the face of one of the pilots killing him instantly. His partner had to fly that gory mess back to base. Before we flew that day, we were given a thorough briefing about the hazards of flying around migratory birds. Avoiding them was the best measure to take.

Zamboni and I flew the first sortie that morning. We took off to the north and made our first turn out of the pattern. As we were climbing through ten thousand feet the sky in front of us suddenly exploded with Sandhill Cranes! There was no time for us to take evasive action and we were on them and through them in less time than it took to write this sentence. We just glanced over at each other, breathed a sigh of relief, and pressed on with our mission.

One other hazard was pure West Texas! It was rattle-snakes. If you went out for a night flight, you were always very careful during your preflight. The base was in a semidesert type area and there were rattlers right there with us. At night, when it got cool, the snakes liked to get on the concrete runways and ramps to stay warm. Sometimes they crawled up in wheel wells of T-37 aircraft. I never saw one during pre-flight, but I saw plenty on the runways at night.

By this time, we were starting to get deeper in Instrument Flying, and one day, Zamboni did something that still amazes me to this day.

I was successfully nailing a Ground Controlled Approach under the hood. Everything was perfect – course, rate of descent, airspeed, etc. I did everything exactly as the controller told me. Usually, in a GCA approach, when you reach minimums, which were 300 feet, the controller says, "Runway should be in sight, take over visually and land."

When we had reached that point, Zamboni said to the controller, "Keep talking us down." Then he said to me, "Keep flying!" He let me fly it all the way to touchdown, completely blinded by the hood.

"Hold this heading and make a touch and go!" I did a touch and go without ever seeing the runway! I can't begin to tell you what that did for my confidence! Like I said earlier, Zamboni always gave me those little "extras" that meant so much.

When it came time for my Instrument Mid-Phase Check Ride I had the bad luck to draw Lieutenant Jerk for my Check Pilot. Jerk had the reputation of being very impatient, and he did everything he could to rattle the student. Everything went fine until I flew a GCA. This was the last maneuver of the check ride, and I felt I had passed it with no problems. He told me to contact Webb Approach Control and request a GCA approach.

When the approach controller instructed me to contact the final controller, he gave me a frequency instead of a pre-set channel. I looked over at the radio, and it was difficult to tell which channel matched that frequency. I made the stupid mistake of asking Lieutenant Jerk what channel that was since he was sitting right in front of the radio.

"Trahan, if you can't see that from where you are sitting, I'm going to wash you out of this program!" I leaned over a little bit and got the frequency myself. I flew a good GCA, but I was so pissed off at him it didn't matter at that point. However, I didn't say anything. He gave me an 81% on the ride. The Standard score was 84%. That was a pretty good score for an instrument mid-phase ride.

After I got back to the table, Zamboni asked me how the ride went, and I told him.

"I see where Jerk gets his reputation."

"Mike, don't say anything to your classmates about how he is. It will just rattle them if they draw him for their check ride."

So, I didn't tell them anything.

We got a few Formation rides in the T-37. Zamboni told us there would be no check ride in formation and to just relax and enjoy it. Relaxing is the key to good formation flying – that and total undivided attention. If you are flying on someone's wing you cannot take your eyes off of his airplane. Bill showed me the reference points on the leader's airplane.

"Keep those points exactly as they are in your vision right now, and you will stay in position. You will have to constantly work the power and the controls to hang in there."

It was fun, and I picked it up pretty well.

T-37's in Formation

After Bill took me on a Cross-Country to Tinker and La-redo, the T-37 program started winding down. We spent a lot of time preparing for our Instrument Final Check. I drew Major Ethun for my check pilot and I made an 82% raw score. I was happy to be done with that phase, but I was also pleased to know I could fly instruments. That was one area where my civilian training was lacking. I just didn't have enough money to go for an instrument rating, so I received only the barest minimum training. Of course, through stu-pidity and poor planning, I had done some flying in instru-ment conditions, and it was very uncomfortable. I was glad to know, if that ever happened again I would now be quali-fied for it.

My check pilot for my Contact Final Checkride was Cap-tain Wihlms. Everything went well until we got to spins. The entry was good, and after four turns, he had me initiate my recovery. The airplane recovered immediately, and then suddenly the nose tried to tuck under. Instinctively I made some quick stick and rudder inputs and it snapped back into a normal dive.

"What the heck was that?" he asked.

"Sir, I don't know! That's the first time I've seen the airplane behave like that. I don't think it was anything I did, and it surprised the heck out of me."

"It was new to me, too. But apparently you did the right thing, because we recovered immediately. That was an excellent spin recovery Lieutenant. Let's go land. Your T-37 training is complete. Congratulations!"

Those words were music to my ears. Next step – The T-38 Talon!

3561st Section Graduates of the T-37 Program

Top Row L/R: Daryl Holsman, Ahmad Separi, John King, Mike Anderson, Dave Kinton, Boyce Core, Mike Trahan, Walt Lawson, "Tex: Thomasson, Paul Baker
Middle Row L/R: Dick Lyle, Jay Saul, Gene Hall, Ira Hester, George D'Angelo, Dick Wright

Bottom Row L/R: Jim Roberts, Allen Boone, Ray Caracciolo, Duane Schroeder, Bob Najaka, Walt Clark.

At the end of the T-37 program we had a nice class party, complete with a band and everything. Sheila Niedzwiecki was there with Allen. I didn't have a date, so I sat with them. Captain Tom Kelly, the 60th Section Leader, stopped by our table. I stood up to greet him and he said, "Congratulations Mike." I asked him what for. He said, "You are Number One in the Class!" To be honest, I was kind of happy Sheila was there to hear that!

Bill and Pat Zamboni invited John King, Boyce Core, and me to their home for dinner the next night. When he met us at the door he said, "Hi, I'm BILL Zamboni!" To that point we always addressed him as Lieutenant Zamboni. Boyce said, "I'm Boyce Core." I said, "I'm Mike Trahan," and John King said "I'm Lieutenant King!" We all got a good laugh out of that.

Bill, Pat, and I had developed a lasting friendship during the time he was my instructor. We had a lot in common. They were both Catholic, and that is an automatic bond for me. I was thrilled when later in the year, they had a son, and they named him Michael after me. We are still friends to this day.

Chapter 5

The T-38 Program

T-38 "Talon"

The T-38 Talon, aka *The White Rocket*, was built by Northrop Aviation. It was a twin-engine, afterburner-equipped aircraft that was capable of supersonic speeds. At the time we were flying it, the Talon held the Time-to-Climb Record over all other Air Force aircraft, including the Lockheed F-104 Starfighter. It was a hot airplane and pure joy to fly, and I still rank the T-38 as my all-time favorite airplane.

Transferring from the T-37 to the T-38 line shack was the easiest move we made at UPT. When we got to the T-38 briefing room we learned that our Flight Commander was Captain Sonny Rockett! Was that a perfect name or what?

Sonny welcomed us and gave us our Instruct Pilot assignments. My IP was First Lieutenant Blank. Lt. Blank (not his real name) was an Air Force Academy graduate and a F-A-I-P (First Assignment Instructor Pilot). My tablemates were Walter Lawson and David Kinton. After our initial welcome and some briefings, we were told to go over to PE (Personal Equipment) and pick up our G Suits, which were basically inflatable chaps that were necessary when flying high G maneuvers. They prevented the blood from pooling in our lower extremities, thereby allowing us to sustain higher G forces without blacking out. We were happy to get them. G Suits were COOL! The question about how well I would be able to tolerate those G forces without experiencing a lot of pain would soon be answered. Since I did not have any trouble in the T-37, I thought my tailbone had healed completely.

The first thing I noticed about the T-38 flight line was that it was so much quieter than the T-37 line. The T-38 at idle was a mere whisper when compared to the Tweet. We still wore our ear protection, but it was a lot more comfortable environment.

Doing a walk around on the T-38 was easier too. The landing gear struts were several feet longer than those on the Tweet, and this allowed us easy access to the bottom of the wings and fuselage. There were thousands of rivets on the 38, and we had to check them all to ensure that none of them were missing or hanging loose.

Normally, the student sits in the front and the IP in the back in the T-38 - except on Instrument Training Flights. On this first flight I sat in the front. I am not sure, but I suspect that my Dollar Ride was Lieutenant Blank's first flight with a student. He appeared to be pretty tense back there and with good reason. The T-38 was difficult to land from the back seat, and I'm sure that was in his mind as we taxied out for takeoff. I could hear tension in his voice.

He lined us up on the centerline of the runway and he ran the throttles up to 100% power. He held the brakes while we checked the engine instruments. After a few seconds, he released them and moved the throttles into the afterburner position. The right afterburner didn't light, and Blank aborted the takeoff. We went back to the ramp and got a spare airplane.

Our takeoff was normal on the second try. About three seconds after the throttles were moved into the afterburner position, we felt a sudden surge forward as they kicked in. Acceleration was incredible. When we rotated for takeoff, the airplane smoothly lifted off. He held it down to about a hundred feet until we accelerated to 400 knots. Then he made a three G pull up to a forty-five degree climb angle. It felt like we were going straight up, and what a thrill it was!

This was a full afterburner climb, and I later learned it was a rare treat.

We came out of afterburner at twenty thousand feet and continued our climb to FL 250. Once we were there, he leveled off and left the throttles at 100%. He told me to watch the airspeed/mach indicator. I remembered all the concern about the Sound Barrier and how it affected airplanes back in the early days. I expected to at least feel something when we went supersonic, but nothing happened. We stopped accelerating at Mach 1.2.

Blank showed me the rapid roll rate of the airplane, which was 420 degrees per second. He let me fly it around a little bit but mainly it was his show. He demonstrated a high sink maneuver, strongly stressing that I keep my feet off the rudders. Any rudder input, while approaching stall speed, could result in a spin, and spins were prohibited in the T38. After about two turns in a spin, the airplane wrapped up so fast that the transverse G's made it impossible for the pilot to bail out.

In the T-38 program we started out in Instrument Training, so my first training flight was an instrument ride. The student sat in the back seat. Instead of a visor, like the one we used in the T-37, we had a canvas hood that completely blanked out the canopy and the windscreen. We were totally enclosed in that canvas cocoon, and all we could see were the flight instruments.

The IP lined up the aircraft on the runway centerline for takeoff. The student made the takeoff totally blind to the outside. We set the heading bug and used the flight director to keep us straight ahead. If we drifted one way or the other the IP would say, "A little left, a little right." Blank made this first takeoff. I guess he wanted me to experience one before I tried it myself. That made sense to me.

We were climbing through ten thousand feet when he said, "You've got the airplane". The instant I took control the airplane started vibrating wildly. It was so violent the pressurized air was leaking out of the canopy.

"What are you doing back there?"

"I'm not doing anything!"

He assumed control of the airplane and started trying to figure out what was wrong. He pulled each engine back to idle one at a time. The vibrations reduced in intensity when he pulled the right one back. We could still feel them though.

Lt Blank was really hyperventilating now. His voice cracked, "I'm going home!"

He declared an emergency and told them we would be coming in on one engine. He left the right engine at idle, and we made a straight in approach and landing.

We later got a maintenance report and learned that a broken hydraulic pump shaft had caused the vibrations. The shaft was wallowing around in its housing, and it could have done a lot of damage, perhaps even causing a fire had Blank not pulled the engine back to idle.

Capt. Rockett said another airplane would be available after this flight period. It was one of the spares they didn't use. Blank decided we would go up again and complete the lesson. We would be flying at night, but I was under the hood, so what did it matter?

Everything went fine during the flight until we got back in the traffic pattern for landing. Then the trouble started. The winds had shifted from south to northeast, and they were quite a bit stronger. The IP always lands when the student is in the back seat so Blank was flying the airplane. It was unusual to land to the north at Webb, since the prevailing winds were usually out of the south. This meant a pitch-out to the right instead of the left.

A lot of things worked against us that night.   On initial I could see the dust rapidly blowing across the runway from right to left, and when Blank made a normal sixty – degree, two - G pitchout and rolled out parallel to the runway, I knew we were in trouble. We were drifting toward the runway on our downwind leg, and, sure enough, when we turned final, we were way too close to the runway. We overshot badly and had to go around. He made three more IDENTICAL pitchouts and approaches, and all of them resulted in over-shoots and go-arounds. On the last one he tried to force the airplane over to the runway, and we were getting danger-ously close to crashing. I was actually reaching for the ejec-tion handles when the RSU Controller sent him around again.

It was beginning to get damn serious up there. We had been airborne an hour and forty minutes, and we were dan-gerously low on fuel. We had to make a full stop landing on our next approach, or we would have to bail out. The winds were so strong at ground level a bailout would most likely have resulted in injuries for both of us.

When we once again were on downwind, I said, "Lieuten-ant, the crosswind is blowing us into the runway. I suggest a wider pattern and a little crabbing into the wind to keep our final turn wide enough so we make it."

"Trahan, I'm flying this damn airplane. You just sit back there, and keep your mouth shut."

"Yes, Sir!" He was mad at me for speaking up, but he took my suggestion anyway and widened his pattern.

When he finally got us on the ground, we had about four hundred pounds of fuel left. Minimum fuel was eight hundred pounds. I wondered if we would have enough to make it to the ramp.

Our next flight was normal, and we got a lot done. It was such a relief after the first three flights I had with him.

However, on March 20 we went up again, and when we tried to check in with Fort Worth Center, our radio failed. We squawked radio failure on our Transponder to alert the controllers that we were NORDO (No Radio). We aborted the mission and landed.

I was beginning to get a little punchy. Four out of my first five flights in the T-38 resulted in either an emergency or an abnormal situation, and I was quickly losing all confidence in my instructor's abilities as an IP and a pilot. I had also begun to wonder if my relationship with this beautiful airplane was jinxed.

I don't remember what I did wrong on my ninth instrument training flight, but Lt Blank didn't like it much, and he flunked me on the ride. This was my first unsatisfactory ride in UPT.

Captain Sonny Rockett was my check pilot on my Instrument Check Ride. Everything went well and I got an 84% on my raw score. Standard score was 85%. I felt much more comfortable with Captain Rockett in the airplane. It was now time for us to start our contact flying, and I would be moving up to the front seat for these rides.

I was delighted to finally be in the front seat, because riding around in that cocoon in the back seat was starting to get very old. This would be my first takeoff in the Talon. Everything went well until I retracted the landing gear. It was very slow to come up, so Lieutenant Blank decided to abort the flight. That was probably a good idea because you don't want landing gear problems in the T-38. A gear up landing was not an option. The belly of the airplane was made of titanium, and titanium scraping along the runway could ignite a fire that is almost impossible to put out. If the gear didn't come down, the only alternative we had was to bail out! When we extended the landing gear, it was slow to come down, but it indicated down and locked, much to our relief. We made an overweight landing and called it a day.

The next ride was okay, except for one problem. I noticed I was unsteady in pitch control on final approach. The control pressures just didn't feel normal. I couldn't figure it out until I realized Lieutenant Blank was riding the controls with me. In an airplane as sensitive as the T-38, that could cause problems. Captain Rockett was in the RSU that day, and he noticed it too.

When I checked the schedule board the next day, I was surprised and a little concerned that I was flying with Captain Rockett.

After we were airborne, he said, "Let's stay in the high pattern and burn fuel down to our landing weight. Then I want you to show me some landings." I asked him if this was some kind of check ride.

"No, but I did notice you were having some pitch problems on final approach yesterday, and I wanted to see why that was happening."

We flew around in the high pattern for fifteen minutes and then entered the traffic pattern. Pitchout was normal, final turn was normal, and once I was on final the nose never moved. It was like I was flying down a rail!

"Well, I didn't see any problems with that one. Let's see you do it again." I did the same thing three times in a row.

"Mike, why are you doing so well today, when yesterday you were bobbling around so much? I don't see anything wrong with the way you fly this airplane."

"Sir, I believe this is the first time I have ever really felt the airplane on final."

"What do you mean?"

"Sir, I think Lt Blank has been riding the controls on final ever since we started Contact Flying."

He perked up. "Oh?"

"Yes, Sir. Can I have a few minutes in private with you after we land?"

"Of course you can."

After we landed, he invited me into his office and shut the door.

"Sir, this is a very delicate matter, and I definitely don't want to cause any trouble, but I have to get this off my chest." I told him about all the flights I had flown with Lt Blank and how he handled them.

Then I said, "Sir, I have zero confidence in him, and I think he feels the same way about me. It is making us both very uncomfortable in the airplane. I am formally requesting a change of instructors."

Captain Rockett thanked me for being so candid and he said, "When you report to the flight line tomorrow, you will have a new instructor."

My new instructor was Captain Chuck Edgar, and I could

not have hand picked a better IP. Chuck was a highly experienced pilot with thousands of hours of flying time, and he was as smooth as anyone I flew with in the Air Force. He had flown C-121 Constellations before coming to ATC.

Chuck was another Zamboni. He was very relaxed in the airplane, and he let the student fly way beyond what most instructors would tolerate. That is the best way to teach someone if you have the skills and the balls to do it.

I don't know if this was pre-arranged or if Colonel Butcher just picked a name off the schedule board, but however it happened, I was picked to fly with our Wing Commander this day. Knowing he was from Lafayette, I think he just picked the first Cajun name on the board!

It was a thrill to get to fly with my World War II Hero. I was a little tense, having so much rank in the airplane with me, but he put me at ease right away. When we got in the airplane, the first thing he did was have me adjust my mirrors so he could see my face.

"I want to see where your eyes are when you fly." I adjusted the mirrors.

"Okay, Trahan, take me out to the practice area and show me what you got!" So, that's what I did.

When we got to the area I did some acrobatics for him. I started out with a Cloverleaf, then a Cuban Eight, and a Loop. He did a couple, and by then, we were down to our landing weight.

"Let's go back to Webb and shoot some landings!"

We were about to enter the outside pattern when I saw a T-38 in front and slightly to the right of us. We were on a collision course.

"Traffic at one o'clock, Sir, I am breaking out."

"I see it!" I pushed the throttles to Military Power and made a steep climbing right turn. I went back out and re-entered the pattern.

I made a couple of landings, and they were pretty good. On my second touch and go I asked him if he would like to make a landing.

"Yes, I would. I've got the airplane!" We came back around, and everything was perfect until we were about two feet above the ground. He just sort of dropped it in from there. It was one of those, not so good, not so bad landings.

In his defense I must say that he didn't fly that often, and the Talon is pretty difficult to land from the back seat. He was in the middle of the touch and go when he said, "Stop laughing Trahan!"

"Sir, I'm not laughing."

"The hell you're not. I can see your eyes and they are laughing. You've got the airplane!"

I made a couple more landings, and then we took it to the

We were both still laughing when we got back to the briefing room. All eyes in the room were on us. We sat down and he started filling out my grade slip.

"How many solo flights do you have under your belt?"

"I haven't soloed yet, Sir."

"Well, you sure are ready to. That was an excellent flight from start to finish."

I thanked him for flying with me, and he said, "It was my pleasure, Mike." Two rides later, I soloed!

This solo was different from any I have made in any other airplane. This time the Instructor didn't go out with me and make the standard three landings, and then get out and let me go. This time Chuck Edgar said, "Trahan, there is a T-38 out there on the ramp waiting for you. Go out there and fly it!" And that was it!

I can't describe how proud I felt taxiing out to the runway for my first solo in that supersonic fighter type airplane. I thought, if I survived this flight, I could honestly say I was one of the "Big Boys."

First solo pilots are required to stay in the traffic pattern the entire flight. Immediately after takeoff we were too heavy to land, so we had to burn down some fuel. After take-off, I climbed to six thousand feet and flew a ten-mile long box pattern around the base. When I reached landing weight, I dropped down to pattern altitude and started making landings. Unfortunately, the traffic pattern was pretty full, and all I could get was five landings. But, that was enough. Even though all I did was fly around a little bit, burn fuel, and make a few landings, this still was one of the most memorable flights of my entire career.

68

We were flying just about every weekday, so by the weekends we were pretty ragged out. But that didn't stop the more enterprising of us in Snoopy Flight! Somehow some of the classmates put together a special event at the Officer's Club. The proceeds would go to pay for part of the cost for our Class Yearbooks. I think Boyce Core and Paul Baker ramrodded this one. They organized a Casino Night at the Officer's Club. That night was the biggest night in the history of that Club. Everyone came. We all dressed up in thirties era casino worker garb, and the ladies dressed like high dollar hookers. It was a FUN night for all.

I continued to fly with Capt Edgar, and things continued to improve for me. One day I went out solo and wanted to shoot some landings to brush up for my upcoming Contact Final Check Ride. I was in the flare for my first landing, and about a foot above the runway, when the mobile controller said, "Round-out, go around." I went to mil power and went around without touching the runway. I requested a closed pattern and got it. Once again, I was just above the runway, and he said, "Round-out, go around" again. This happened on every landing that period.

The controller was Lt Dave VanBraune, and he was messing with me. He let me get a little closer on each landing and then gave me a go around. On my last go around I said, "Hangover 19 on the go, min fuel, request a closed pattern, and a full stop." This time he let me land. I had gone around twelve times!

When VanBraune came into the briefing room, I went over to his table. I said, "Lieutenant VanBraune, was there something wrong with my approaches out there? Is that why you kept sending me around?"

"Aw, hell no, Trahan, they were all perfect. I just wanted to see how close you could get and go around without touching. You never touched! Besides, why use up rubber on the tires when we both know the landings would have been squeakers."

On July 15 Captain Edgar put me up for my Contact Final check ride with Major Eby, the Chief of T-38 Check Section. Everything went right on that ride for me. My last landing was a roll-on and Major Eby even said wow! As we taxied in he said, "You are working on a 100% excellent ride Trahan. Let's see how you do on emergency procedures!"

Dammit! Why did there always have to be a little suspense in everything I did? I snapped out the first three procedures he asked me, and then he said, "What is the procedure for engaging the barrier?"

"Max aerodynamic breaking to 100 knots and then apply max wheel breaking until prior to engaging the barrier."

"Nope, that's wrong!"

I about shit my pants. Emergency procedures had to be absolutely correct, or you failed. I went through it again, and I could not figure out what was wrong.

"You forgot to say max wheel breaking until JUST prior to engaging the barrier. Too bad, you only get a 97% on this ride!" He gave me a grade of Excellent for the flight.

At this point in the program, I had the highest grades in the class in all phases of flying, and I was neck and neck with Allen Boon for first place in academics. I was skating my way to Top Gun in the class.

I took my first formation ride with Lieutenant Bruce. It was a lot of fun and a lot more involved than formation in the T-37 because we did a lot more. We learned fingertip formation, close trail, extended trail, and pitchout and rejoins in the first phase. I caught on to it right away, and most of my formations grades were excellent. However, I was having a problem. We pulled a lot more G's in formation, and when you are on the wing, you have no choice but to pull as many or more G's than lead if you want to stay in position with him. My tailbone was killing me!

I don't remember why I was switched over to Captain William D. R. Lund's table, but I was. I walked into the briefing room one day, and Captain Edgar said, "Mike, they have assigned you to one of our new instructors."

At that point I didn't know that Lund was a Captain. My first thought was, *Oh crap, not another First Assignment IP?* I should not have been concerned. Bill Lund was a great instructor and a pleasure to fly with. I finished out the program at his table. My final tablemates were Walt Lawson and Dave Kinton.

I flew with Captain Jake Sorenson on my first T-38 Cross Country. Jake was from the Academics Section. We flew from Webb to England AFB in Alexandria, Louisiana, on the first leg. We had just crossed Leon a VORTAC at Flight Level 310 when Jake requested a descent to lower airspace. Houston Center cleared us to 10,000 feet. Jake had me do a rapid descent to 10,000, and then he took control of the airplane. He canceled IFR and dropped us down to a thousand feet above the ground and started making a bunch of wild heading changes. After a few minutes of this he said, "Okay Mike, where are we?"

I looked to my left and recognized *Steinhagen Reservoir*, and straight ahead of us was Jasper, Texas, the home of two of my best friends from The University of Texas. I rolled the airplane to the left and said, "That's Steinhagen Reservoir, and that dam is simply called Dam B. The town off our nose is Jasper, known as the Jewel of The Forest. Jasper has an airport where a beautiful P-51 is based. A doctor owns it. The next town we will come to is Burkeville."

"How in the hell do you know all that?"

"Sir, if we were a little higher we could look to the right and see my hometown. It's about fifty miles to the south of us. I have hunted all over these woods. You got me "lost" in my old stomping grounds!"

He started laughing and said, "Well, so much for that! Let's climb back up to 10,000 and head for England."

I don't remember what we did on the way back to Big

Spring, but that part of the trip was not memorable for anything. It was a nice trip. That T-38 could really cover a lot of ground in a short amount of time. Our time from Big Spring to Alexandria was and hour and twenty-five minutes, and the leg back home was and hour and thirty.

On July 29 I went up on back-to-back flights. They were both formation rides. I flew the first one with Captain Lund. On the second hop I flew solo and Captain Lund flew with another student in the other airplane. It felt pretty cool doing that!

I really embarrassed myself in the Flight Simulator one day. I went over there to fly a simple Instrument Training Flight. I was flying multiple approaches, and was on my third approach when I noticed the airspeed was at zero! I thought there was something wrong with the airspeed indicator, or the simulator had frozen, but that was not the problem. I had taken my eyes off the instruments and was looking at the approach plate, and I let the airplane fly itself into the ground! I raised the canopy and looked over at the link instructor.

"Did I really do that?"

He said, "I'm afraid so Lieutenant!" I had failed the damn link session.

I didn't think it was a big deal, but when I got back to the Line Shack, I found out it was a very big deal. I had to go back over there, that same day, and redo the ride. That Pink Slip had to be cleared before I could continue in the program. It really bothered me that I flew that thing into the ground. I wondered if I might someday do that in a real airplane?

My next flight was a solo formation ride. George D'Angelo and Dave VanBraune were in the other airplane. We were having a great time, and I was hanging in there with them pretty good. George signaled me to go close trail, and I got on his tail. I felt us accelerating, and I knew this was going to be tough. Sure enough, George pulled up into a five G loop and a sudden surge of pain hit my rear end. I tried to reach down and put my hand under my butt cheek to relieve some of the pressure, and in doing so, I got out of position. It was almost impossible to get back into position in close trail when you are on the backside of a loop. I tried, but I just couldn't get there. I called, "Two's Out!" I did that so they would know I was out of position. I had to suffer the indignity of flying back to the traffic pattern by myself. When we got on the ground, Dave asked me what happened.

"I just got too far out of position when you started downhill on that loop." He just laughed, "Pussy!" I didn't mention anything about my ass hurting so bad I could hardly stand it.

That flight got me to wondering if I wanted to, or even could, spend the rest of my career in fighters where pulling heavy G's was a way of life.

I had the great good fortune to fly with Chuck Edgar for my long cross-country. He picked a couple of terrific bases for us to visit. On the first leg we flew nonstop from Webb to Williams AFB in Chandler, Arizona, a suburb of Phoenix.

It was a hot summer day in West Texas, and when we approached the New Mexico border, we encountered a broken line of thunderstorms. We were cruising at Flight Level 410, and it appeared we could top the storms. We started a climb to Flight Level 490, and I watched the cumulonimbus clouds grow as we approached them. They were out-climbing us! We abandoned our attempt to top them and leveled off at Flight Level 450. We were able to circumnavigate all of them, and soon we were doing a Jet Penetration Approach into "Willie!"

The next morning Chuck and I flew over to George AFB in California. It was a short hop, but we needed three destinations on this trip. We refueled at George and headed for Nellis AFB in Las Vegas, Nevada. As the crow flies, George to Nellis was just a thirty or forty minute hop, but Chuck had something else in mind. He showed me our route on the World Aeronautical Chart. We would take off from George and fly north up California's Imperial Valley until we got abeam Death Valley. We would go low level and just enjoy the view. When we were even with Death Valley, we hopped over the mountains and dropped down again. We went screaming over that famous desert at 500 knots! I'm sure we were not the first T-38 to do that.

When we got to Vegas, Chuck said, "We are going downtown tonight!" He sounded pretty excited. It turned out Chuck was a pretty accomplished gambler, and he had spent a tour at Nellis earlier in his career. He knew his way around that town.

We went straight to a casino, and Chuck started playing craps. I didn't have any money I wanted to lose, and I didn't gamble. I just walked around checking out the drink girls and catching the free lounge shows. An hour later, I was pretty bored. I went back to the table where Chuck was gambling.

"I'm getting kind of hungry. Will you be here much longer?"

"Mike, I'm on a pretty good roll. I'll tell you what, if you give me another hour, I will treat us both to a night on the town with my winnings."

I thought, *"Yeah, sure. He will be tapped out, and we will have to hitchhike back to the damn base!"* I was wrong.

Chuck won over three hundred dollars that night, and he did treat me to a nice night in Vegas. We went to a great buffet for dinner where I had lobster and prime rib. After that, we went to the "Lido de Parie" show at the Stardust Casino. After the show, Chuck gave me some money for a cab ride back to the base. He said he wanted to stay and gamble some more. I don't know what time he got in that night, but he sure looked sleepy the next morning.

I did all the flight planning for this leg of the trip, and when I looked at the chart, I saw our departure was going to take us north of the Grand Canyon. I asked Chuck if it would be possible to detour off course and take a look at the Canyon, and he replied, "Sure it is, Mike. In fact, Air Traffic Control will be expecting that request from you. Just plan a direct course from the Canyon to Alamogordo, New Mexico, and then on in to Webb." I did as he said. The detour would not cost us much fuel at all.

On taxi out, I could tell Chuck was barely hanging in there with me. I read back our IFR clearance and checked in with Nellis Tower for takeoff. Tower asked, "Webb 69, will you be requesting the Canyon Tour?"

"Affirmative, if it's available."

"Webb 69, you are cleared for takeoff. Turn right to heading 150 and climb to fifteen thousand. Contact departure when airborne. Come back and see us again!"

Departure control vectored me over the Canyon. It was absolutely spectacular. I don't think I will ever forget that sight. By that time Chuck was sound asleep, but I didn't wake him because I knew he had seen it many times before.

As we reached the eastern end of the Canyon, Departure Control said, "Webb 69, climb to FL230 and contact Los Angeles Center."

Center then cleared me to FL410 and gave me a vector direct to Webb AFB. We must have had a hundred knot tailwind because we were at Webb in no time.

I made a jet penetration and was entering the traffic pattern when I remembered Chuck was back there. I thought about going ahead and landing without waking him, but then I realized, if something went wrong on landing, I would be putting his life in jeopardy. As I entered Initial, I said, "Captain Edgar, it's time to wake up."

A couple of seconds later he said, "Where are we?"

"We are on initial at Webb!" He had slept like a baby the entire way.

My next two flights were with Captain Lund. We were tuning up for my Formation Mid-Phase Check Ride. I got an excellent on one of them and a good on the other. At this point in the program I was on top of the world. I could see the end coming up, and I was solidly in the Number One position in the class. That was a goal I cherished from day one, and the next day I took my Formation Mid-Phase check.

T-38 Two-Ship Formation

I drew Captain Bob for the check pilot on my Formation Mid-Phase ride. I was doing my pre-flight checks and trying to be as meticulous as possible. I was in the middle of my cockpit check, and apparently, he didn't like the pace of my work.

"Come on Trahan, don't take all day. We've got another airplane waiting for us." So, I picked up the pace.

Everything appeared normal until our formation was in the number one hold position to take the runway. We had already closed the canopies when Bob exclaimed, "I'm not believing this!"

"What's wrong, Sir?"

"Take a look at the fuel gauge!"

My heart literally sank. We had only 700 pounds of fuel in the airplane. It had not been refueled for this flight, and I missed it on my pre-flight. We had just about enough to get off the ground, flame out, and bail out. I knew in that instant that I had already failed this Check Ride. Now it was just a matter of how bad it was going to be. I really wanted to shut down the airplane and call it a day, but I couldn't.

Bob told our wingman that we were going to have to go back to the ramp. They said they would wait on the north end of the ramp for us. As we taxied back and refueled, I could tell things were getting pretty tense between Bob and me. I knew I had really messed up. It took them about ten minutes to fuel us and we taxied back out to the runway.

I made the takeoff on the wing, and I hung in there pretty good. We did a pitchout and rejoin, and that went okay too. Then lead signaled close trail. I put us in the slot, and soon we were accelerating for a loop. I stuck my pitot tube as close to their tailpipes as humanly possible because I did not want to risk getting out of position.

As we were just topping out in the loop, he said, "You're too close, Trahan, back it off a little." Well, I backed it off, just as lead started down the backside of the loop. Lead was accelerating at the same time I was decelerating, and I realized I was already out of position. I had never done this in an airplane before, but I just gave up! We were wallowing around in the sky and running out of airspeed. Lead was leaving us like a rocket, and I just didn't give a shit.

Bob said, "Dammit, I've got the airplane!" He took over and recovered from the unusual attitude I had left us in.

We did some extended trail, and that is a maneuver that takes a lot of patience. I found myself not closing as fast as I wanted to, and I jerked the airplane around a little bit. Another expletive came from the back seat. I'm glad we changed leads at that point. I probably would have rammed the other airplane if this had gone much further. Bob didn't say another word all the way back to the base.

When we got to the briefing room, we both sat down.

"Well, what do you think about that ride?"

I was embarrassed, disappointed, heartbroken, and I was pretty flustered. I have relived that conversation a thousand times since then, and there are so many other things I could have said. I should have said, "Sir, I owe you an apology. That was the worst flight I have had since I started this program. In fact, it's the worst flight I have ever flown." Unfortunately, I didn't say that. Instead, I said -

"I thought it was Shit Hot!"

Well, that did it. Now he was really pissed off. Of all the stupid responses I could have made at that moment, I picked the worst possible one. He got out his pencils and started working on my grade slip. The first one that came out was the red one. He colored a little triangle in the lower right corner of the grade slip, and my Pink (Failure) was official. The only question left was how low would the grade be? Well, it was a 66%! I think I made the lowest grade in the class on the Formation Mid-Phase check. Not only that, I had failed a Check Ride. That meant my next check ride would be an ELIMINATION RIDE! I had come this far, and done so well, and now I was facing washing out! I also knew I could kiss my Top Gun award goodbye.

I was physically sick! I imagined the 60th Section cheered when they heard the news. Fred Parrott had been breathing down my neck all year, and now he had his opening. All he had to do was fly a decent ride, and he would pass me up!

I don't remember much about the rest of that day, but I do remember thinking, *"Why do I always get so close to my goals in life, only to get knocked flat on my ass right before they happen?"* I had thought I was going to be a kicker for the varsity at Ole Miss during my sophomore year, but then I broke my damn toe one week before the first game. And now THIS had happened.

One of my most vivid memories of this day was shaving. I kept looking in the mirror and wondering if this was going to be my last day in UPT. It was all I could do to keep from throwing up. I remember that my hands were very cold. I don't know what physiological response caused that, but I'm sure it was just plain old raw nerves.

I had the good fortune of getting Major Eby for this ride. He was the same pilot who gave me the Contact Final that I had done so well on. When we sat down, he said, "What are we doing here, Trahan? I could not believe it when they told me what happened on your Check Ride. Now let's go out there and get this out of the way!"

I took off on the wing, and I was so tense I could hardly fly.

"Let me fly the airplane a few minutes Mike. Just relax and fly like I know you can, and this will be fine."

"Major Eby, I have never been this nervous in an airplane. I can't believe I've gotten myself in this position."

"Everything will be fine!"

As soon as we got in the practice area lead put me in trail. Instead of a loop, lead did a Cloverleaf. I hung in there like #4 on the Thunderbirds.

Eby said, "Now why didn't you do it like that two days ago?"

I didn't say anything. We did a short version of extended trail, and I held position perfectly.

"Okay, that's enough for me. Now signal him to take the

wing. We need to fly a check ride for the student in that airplane."

When we got back to the briefing room, I felt like someone had just lifted a thousand pound weight off my chest. The ride was not graded. It was just pass or fail. And, Thank You, God, I passed!

During this time, Sheila's roommate Donna and I had been dating all summer, and we had developed a close relationship. It was a little too close for me. At that point in my life, I just was not ready to settle down. I knew, depending on my assignment, I would most likely go to Vietnam. It was just a matter of when. I told Donna that, and she didn't take it too well. I didn't see her again. Sheila and Allen were also having their problems and they broke up too. We didn't see Sheila again either.

The next couple of weeks were spent flying formation rides with a little contact flying thrown in. We did some four-ship formation, and that was pretty interesting. The coolest part of the entire flight was coming in as a four ship and pitching out in sequence for a landing.

On September 13, I took my Final Formation Check ride. Most of this ride was about flying the wing on approaches and missed approaches.

That must have been a Friday the 13th because luck was not with me that day. I drew the Deputy Wing Commander for my check pilot. To make matters worse, my old buddy Captain Bob was the check pilot in the other airplane. I knew I was, as they say in the business, screwed!

The student in the other airplane was one of our weaker formation students, and I knew it. At this point I just wanted to get through the damn thing, so I flew the smoothest lead I possibly could so he could stay with me. He did a good job as lead too.

When we landed, both of our check pilots were livid. Mine said, "Boy, you two guys sure *mothered* each other up there today. You were practically holding hands."

"Sir, we just wanted to pass this ride!" He gave me a Good on my grade, but scored me a 62%. It was now official. I had made the worst grades in the class in formation. That pretty much ripped it for me.

We had a final check ride in the T-38 Simulator too. I made a 92.6% on that one. Even though it was in the Link, that score buoyed my spirits a little bit.

At this point, I believe, I was leading in Academics as well. Section mate Allen Boone was right there with me. Allen really wanted the Academic Award. It killed him every time I outscored him on an exam. I stumbled badly on the Instrument Procedures and Radio Aids test. I think I made the mistake of reading too much into the questions, and I barely passed the test. Our last exam was in Weather. To be honest, I think I let up on that last course. I made a fair grade, but it was not enough. Boone passed me up.

We were getting close to graduation now, and we were getting a taste of what it was going to be like in the "Real Air Force". Six of us were scheduled to fly a Day/Night Cross Country to Barksdale AFB in Shreveport, Louisiana. We took off late in the afternoon, and we flew from Big Springs to Abilene to Fort Worth to Shreveport. We filed and flew an IFR flight plan.

When I flew over Redbird field that day, I thought about Clyde Jetton and the folks down at Jet Aero. That was the place I went after college graduation, thinking I would get to do some charter flying, and I wound up being a Line Boy instead. I wished old Clyde could have seen me then!

We were in Base Operations in Shreveport, doing our flight planning for the leg back to Big Spring, when one of the IP's came in and said, "Men, for all intents and purposes, you are Air Force Pilots. And, in honor of that near distinction you have, I want you to depart this place like Fighter pilots. I want you to do FULL AFTERBURNER CLIMBS to 20, 000 feet! You think you pussies can do that without embarrassing me?" Oh man, talk about license to steal.

We did exactly as the IP told us, and we looked GOOD! I was number five to take off, and it was such a thrill watching my classmates blasting nearly straight up into the night sky in full glorious afterburner. The flame from their tailpipes appeared to be fifty feet long. When it came my turn I lit the burners, lifted off, held the airplane down at one hundred feet above the ground until I hit 450 Knots, and then I pulled hard to near vertical. I zoomed up to 19,000 feet and then rolled one hundred eighty degrees and pulled again. I leveled off, inverted, at exactly 20, 000 feet! I rolled back upright and turned on course to Abilene.

As I was approaching Dyess AFB in Abilene, I could see the rotating beacon of the T-38 in front of me. It was Bob Najaka, and he appeared to be turning off course. I heard him call Fort Worth Flight Service and tell him he was diverting to Dyess.

I keyed my mike and whispered, *"Hey, Bob, is that you?"*

"Yes, it is!"

"What are you doing?"

Fort Worth FSS broke in and said, "Is someone calling Fort Worth?"

We ignored him. He whispered back, *"I'm landing at Dyess, Mike, I've got a fuel problem!"*

"Do you want me to follow you in?"

The IP behind me broke in and said, "Hangover 19, you continue to home base. I'll follow him in."

So, I did what he told me.

Bob had gotten a little disoriented during his afterburner climb and leveled out at 10, 000 feet instead of 20,000. He had gone quite a ways at the lower altitude before he realized his mistake, and then he snuck up to 20,000. It was too late. At 10,000 the fuel burn was quite a bit higher than at 20,000, and he ran short. The IP reported that Bob's airplane was venting fuel, and that's why he was short.

The next night a bunch of us went on a solo round robin cross-country. We flew from Webb over Wink and Roswell and Lubbock and Abilene and back to Big Springs. We flew at Flight Level 410, and I could see the entire route. I remember one specific moment of that flight. I had just leveled off at 410 and settled down into cruise. I turned the instrument lights as low as I could, and still be able to read them. Then I looked up at the stars above. It was a crystal clear night, and I felt like I was almost there amongst the stars instead of below them. I said a little prayer, thanking God for allowing me to have my dream. I knew then I was going to graduate, and I knew He had been with me all the way.

This was one of the best rides of the entire year. We planned a low level route that took us out over the boondocks. We were flying at 500 feet and we wanted to avoid populated areas as much as possible. Bill Lund was my IP on this flight. We flew strictly by pilotage and map reading. Our checkpoints were planned down to the second. Our objective was to "bomb" the Goodyear Test Track just north of San Angelo. When I made my turn at the bomb run IP (Initial Point), I realized I was three seconds late. I lit the afterburners and hit my TOT (Time Over Target) on the second! I did a six G pull up and that's when I realized I had not planned the route from San Angelo to Big Spring. I looked down and saw Highway 87 below us and lined up with it to get started. Then I tuned the BGS VORTAC and headed home. Bill gave me an Excellent on that ride.

I drew Colonel Wahl for my cross-country check ride. He was the 3561st Squadron Commander, and he was a big ole nice guy. We flew from Webb to Bergstrom AFB, in Austin, on the day portion of the trip. Ironically, that was the very day Charles Gregory Whitman climbed the University of Texas tower and shot up a bunch of people.

On the return leg we did a GCA and a missed approach at Dyess AFB and then flew on into Big Spring. Everything went extremely well, and I passed with a raw score of 92%. I also got an Excellent for the ride. It was a great way to finish up after all my anguish over my formation fiasco.

A week later a representative from the FAA came to our Flight Shack. Anybody who wanted to could get their Commercial Pilot's License and Instrument Rating all based on the training we had gotten at UPT. I believe the guys had to take an exam on FAR's to get theirs. I already had my Commercial Ticket, so I walked up to the FAA guy and showed it to him. I said, "What do I have to do to get an instrument rating tacked onto this thing?" He smiled and said, "Here, give it to me." I handed him my license, and he wrote out a brand new temporary one for me. He handed it to me and said, "Congratulations, Lieutenant, you are now an FAA Instrument Rated Pilot!" I wish I had asked him to add a T-37 and a T-38 Type Rating on it too.

About a week before graduation we were all scheduled for one last solo flight in the T-38. There was really no reason for this flight. All our training was done and we had nothing else to prove. I think this solo ride was a graduation present from the staff at Webb. The only thing our IP's told us before we took off was, "Don't go out there and do anything stupid!"

So, we all went out there and did stupid things.

We had been told that there were two things we could not do in the T-38. We were not supposed to fly at or above Mach 1, and we had to remain below 50, 000 feet. That day we all became members of the "Ten Mile Mach Buster's Club"

I took off before sunrise on that flight just so I could enjoy one more of those spectacular events out there in flier's paradise. I was climbing through FL450 as the sun broke the horizon. It was magnificent. I was a qualified Air Force Jet Pilot, and it felt so good.

After accelerating to Mach 1.1 at FL450, I zoomed the airplane up to FL 510, slowly rolled inverted, and gently moved the control stick aft. When the nose was pointed straight down, I went to idle power, popped the speed brakes, and dropped back down to FL250. I told Fort Worth Center I was going to stay in the area a few minutes and do some acrobatics. He said the area was all mine.

I did cloverleafs, Cuban eights, loops, rolls, and just danced all over the sky. I sang and talked to myself as I flew.

I sang songs like, "Climb Every Mountain" and "The High and The Mighty." Once I looked at myself in the mirrors and said, "You are one shit-hot jet pilot!" And then, way too soon, it was time to land.

I keyed my microphone to check out of the practice area. I noticed the mike switch felt a little funny, and I keyed it again.

"Fort Worth, Webb 69 – Home Plate!"

"Webb 69, you are cleared to Home Plate, and be advised your microphone has been stuck for the last ten minutes. We heard EVERYTHING you said, sang, and did!"

"What can I say? I love to fly!"

"Son, that is apparent to everyone in Fort Worth Center! This tape is going to be a classic around here!"

I could hear laughter behind him. He wasn't kidding. Everyone at Fort Worth Center had been listening in to my little performance! A couple of minutes later, he said, "Webb 69, when are you graduating?"

I told him in one week. I said this was my last flight in the T-38.

"Congratulations, it's been a real pleasure working with you."

"Thank you, Forth Worth, I appreciate you watching out for me too. We'll talk again!"

The traffic pattern was a madhouse. Snoopy Flight was tearing it up. Paul Baker was doing aileron rolls on downwind, and we were ripping around that base like a bunch of banshees. On my last approach I patted the airplane on the glare shield, and said, "Thanks Sweetheart. I'll never forget you!"

"Tiger Shot"

A short time before graduation we were given a list a list of aircraft assignments to choose from. Our class standing determined which assignment we got. We were told to list all the assignments according to our preference, from first to last. If our chosen assignment was still available when our name came up, it was ours.

I agonized over this decision. When I got to Webb, I

wanted to be what every one of us wanted to be – A Fighter Pilot! As time progressed I was more certain of that goal. Then I crashed that link and busted that formation check ride. That shook my confidence as a fighter pilot. I also considered a few other things when making this once in a lifetime decision.

In spite of the fact that it had been over three years since my cyst operation, my tailbone still hurt like hell when I experienced a lot of G forces. I knew, if I flew a fighter, I would be flying in a high G environment job for the rest of my career. I was not sure I could stand that.

I had never really been any place but Orange, Texas, and I wanted to see the world. I knew, as a fighter pilot, I would see some parts of it, but not as many as I would as a transport pilot.

I was torn between fighters and transports for another reason. I had always had such great admiration for the Air Force Pilot who flew Air Force One. In my wildest dreams, I envisioned myself as that person. The only path to that job was flying for the Airlift Command.

One day my roommate Jim Roberts asked me what I wanted to fly when we graduated, and I flippantly replied, "I want to fly Air Force One! He laughed for five minutes.

Jim was in for a big and ironic surprise later in his career. His first assignment was a C-123 in Vietnam. His second assignment was a C-141 at Norton AFB in California. His third assignment was to a Special Airlift Missions (SAM) Squadron based at Andrews AFB in Washington D.C. His airplane was a VC-137 – which was a highly modified Boeing 707. He became the Copilot on the airplane that flew President around.

He said he never got to fly it under its Air Force One desig-nation (President on board), but he did fly the same airplane on other missions.

I was high enough in the class to have either a fighter or transport assignment. I weighed all those considerations, and it came down to a coin toss. I made two lists. One of the lists went as follows: *F-100, F-101, F-102, F-105, and F-4C.* The other list had only one airplane: the *C-141 Starlifter* jet transport. I flipped a coin. Heads, I would fly fighters. Tails, I would fly transports. It came up tails! And, that's how I chose. I got the C-141.

In retrospect, I must say that passing up my chance to fly fighters was one of the biggest mistakes of my life! I know my choice surprised and disappointed a lot of people. My buddy Glen Doss almost disowned me over it.

I invited a few people to my graduation. Of course, Mom and Dad were first on the list. I also invited Lt. Col Benjamin F. Sellars and his wife Louise. Ben was the first Regular Air Force Officer I got to know personally. He was my buddy Don Walker's uncle. I also invited my Civilian Flight Instructor Edward Feuge and his son Randy. I had to think long and hard before I came up with my last invitee.

I still had no steady girlfriend, and I regretted that I didn't have anyone special in my life to share this wonderful event with. So, I chose the girl I admired the most - I invited my cousin Ann Foreman! Ann rode out with Mom and Dad. I was so glad she was there to share this with me.

Dad, Ben, Ed, and Randy attended the all-male Dining In the night before graduation. I was so proud to have them all there with me. The Dining In was great.

There were numerous toasts offered, and one of them

was to me for my role as "Whisper Control." Apparently the story, about Najake and me over Abilene that night, had made the rounds at Webb AFB. Then Colonel Butcher got up to give out some awards.

The first one announced was the most coveted one – The Commander's Trophy or Flying Training Award. This was given to the student who had the highest average in the Flight Training Phase. The recipient was Emmons F. Parrott! Fred was the guy I noticed on our first day at Webb.

The Academic Award went to Allen W. Boone.

The third award was the Outstanding Officer Award. David Kinton got that one.

There was one more award, and I didn't even know it existed. It was the Distinguished Graduate Award. It was given to a student who maintained a 90 or above average in all phases of Flight Training. I received that one.

At that point it really didn't matter any more. I was just happy to know that, in about twelve hours, I would be getting my Certificate of Aeronautical Rating – Jet Pilot, and I would have a shiny new set of Wings to pin onto my uniform!

Receiving Outstanding Officer Graduate Award

Class 67C graduated on October 22, 1966. Out of the 65 men who started out with us the previous October, only 45 of us got our wings. Major Butler's prediction that only two thirds of the class would graduate held true.

After Colonel Butcher gave me my Certificate of Aeronautical Rating, Colonel Roland handed me my Silver Wings.

When all the wings were handed out, Snoopy Flight was dismissed.

Colonel Chester J. Butcher hands me my Certificate of Aeronautical Rating – Jet Pilot

There was just one more formality left, and this was the one I had been looking forward to since the day I got to Webb. I walked over to Mom and Dad, and I handed Mom my wings. Dad beamed as she pinned them on for me. It was, without a doubt, the proudest moment of my life!

Mom pins on my wings while Dad Looks on

It was a little bit anti-climactic when my Pilot Training Class disbanded and disbursed. There were no going away parties and we didn't go around saying goodbye to each other either. I think, after being together up to sixteen hours a day for an entire year, we had seen enough of each other.

It felt strange to me, but that's the way Air Force life is. There are many departures but few goodbyes. Besides, we knew the odds were good that we would be crossing paths again. I was certain that two of my classmates and I would see each other. Mike Anderson and Ray Caracciolo also got C-141 assignments. In fact, Ray and I were going to be squadron mates. We were assigned to the 76th Military Airlift Squadron based at Charleston AFB, S.C. Anderson was assigned to a base in California.

My orders said to report to Tinker AFB in the middle of November, for my Initial C-141 Training. I had some time to kill, so I made the most of it. I loaded all my things in my car and checked out of the Bachelor Officer's Quarters. I went by to see two of my IP's, Bill Zamboni and Bill Lund, before I left.

I drove to Orange that same day. Dad greeted me warmly when I walked into the family room. He said he was proud of me and that felt so good! I walked into the kitchen, and there was Mom, stirring a roux for a pot of shrimp gumbo. When we embraced she said again, for the ump-teenth time, "I'm proud of you too, Mike!" I said, "You know what Mom? I'm proud of me too!" We both laughed.

I had a very nice visit home this time. We three spent a lot of time talking about the future. I said I would be flying worldwide routes out of Charleston, and that a lot of my trips would probably be in and out of Vietnam. I added that I would do some flying in Europe too. I told them I had two weeks off before I had to report to Tinker AFB.

My two weeks in West Orange flew by. It was time for me to drive to Oklahoma City. I said goodbye to my parents, and Dad was there this time. I told them I had no idea when I would get to see them again, but I felt like it would be quite some time. I left them each a Christmas present. I bought watches for both of them in the Webb Base Exchange.

I had to go through Dallas on my way to Oklahoma City and I left early so I could spend a night there. I wanted to visit Donna and tie up what I thought were some loose ends between us. I called ahead to see if she would be home and she said she would.

When I got to her apartment that day I told her I was sorry that our break-up had to happen on the phone and she said she was over being mad at me.

"Donna, you just don't seem very comfortable today. Is

something the matter?"

"Mike, I've been seeing a guy and I think he might be the one. His name is Bill, and he is a fellow teacher. He knows about you, and I don't think he would like that you are here."

I congratulated her and wished her luck and as I was leaving I asked her to tell Sheila hello for me.

"Sheila is on a Braniff trip, I'll let her know you were here, Mike. Where are you staying?" I told her and then I left.

I was tired from the long drive and the visit with Donna, so as soon as I got to the motel, I went to bed. I was sleeping soundly when I heard a knock at the door. I glanced at my watch. It was three o'clock in the morning! I went to the door and looked through the peephole. It was Sheila.

There she stood, resplendent in her Braniff uniform, designed by Pucci. It was a very sexy outfit, and even though she had been flying half the night, she looked great. She said, "Well, don't just stand there in your drawers! Get dressed. You are taking me to breakfast!"

We talked for two hours, and the names Allen and Donna only came up once. She asked about his aircraft assignment, and I told her he got F-4's.

She said, "Great, that's what he wanted."

I told her about going to see Donna, and she told me a little bit about Donna's boyfriend Bill.

"Well, she sure got over me fast!" Sheila laughed.

Other than that, our conversation never included them again. It was just a very nice visit between two friends. I had no idea if this would lead to anything or not, but I had spent enough time with Sheila to know she was a great girl, and I hoped I would see her again. When we parted she said,

"Keep in touch Mike, and let me know where you are." I said I would.

Chapter 6

Flying The C-141 Starlifter

The Lockheed C-141 was the most modern transport airplane in the Air Force fleet. It had only been flying a couple of years when I got to it. The 76th Military Airlift Squadron was still getting brand new airplanes. Until recently, the crews for the 141's were drawn from experienced MAC pilots. My class was the third one to go straight from Undergraduate Pilot Training to C-141's.

The C-141 was a high-winged T-tailed aircraft with four jet engines and a cruising speed of Mach .74. It flew at the higher altitudes. Most of the C-141 missions lasted eight to ten hours. The cargo was loaded from the rear ramp, which was accessed through two giant clamshell doors. It could carry up to 70,000 pounds of cargo. Our takeoff gross weight was 316,700 pounds. War Emergency Gross Weight was 325,000 pounds.

The standard crew on the C-141 consisted of the Aircraft Commander, Copilot, Navigator who were all officers, and a Flight Engineer and two Loadmasters, all enlisted men.

As I drove up to Tinker AFB, I realized how huge that base was. I checked into the Training Squadron, got my schedule, and then checked into the VOQ. My apartment there was a lot nicer than the one I had at Webb. I had a roommate. His name was John something, and he was a Captain. John was transitioning from C-124's to C-141's.

The next morning I started Ground School, and I soon learned that the systems on the C-141 were a lot more complex than those on any other airplane I had flown. Learning my first Transport Category airplane was quite a challenge. I did well enough in class. I just wanted to get through it and get my hands on that airplane.

My classmate Ray Caracciolo was there too. Somehow he wound up in school a couple of weeks ahead of me. That meant he had no time off between UPT graduation and reporting to Tinker. Ray had also been assigned to the 76th.

Right before Thanksgiving I called Sheila Niedzwiecki. I invited her to come up for Thanksgiving. She thanked me for the invitation but declined. She said she had a prior commitment. Once again she told me to stay in touch with her.

At the end of Ground School we got two rides in the C-141 Flight Simulator. There were hundreds of switches to learn and we had to know the function of each one. Each of the two simulator sessions lasted four hours each. We were pretty familiar with the C-141 cockpit by the time we flew our first training flight.

After we finished ground school we met our Instructors. Mine was Major George W. Mizell. Majors were not that common in ATC, so I was a little intimidated by his rank. I said, "I'm pleased to meet you Major Mizell!"

"Welcome to the REAL Air Force Mike, and my name is George. Call me that." That put me at ease with him right away.

George had just my roommate John and me as students. Since John was senior in rank he had the choice of going first or second on this training flight. He surprised me and chose to go second. That meant that on my first ride in this giant airplane I would be at the controls.

John and I had practiced the checklist in the simulator dozens of times, so it felt pretty natural to be going through it for real now. George sat in the right seat and read it to me. I moved the switches to their proper position and responded. It all went pretty smoothly. The checklist responses had to be precisely what was written and I only missed a few of them.

After engine start George said I had to do all the taxiing because the nose wheel steering wheel was on my side of the cockpit.

"Mike, steering is very sensitive and this is a big ole long airplane. Any jerky inputs to that wheel will be magnified throughout the airplane. I don't want you jerking me around!" I can't tell you how many times he said, "He jerked me John!"

George said our initial rotation was five to ten degrees nose up. It was a gradual thing. He told me to be slow and smooth when I rotated, and the airplane would take care of the rest. He also admonished me to keep in mind that the maximum allowed takeoff pitch attitude was thirteen degrees. It had something to do with the high wing blanking out the T tail elevators.

I felt like an airline captain sitting up there in the left seat of that magnificent aircraft, and I was surprised how easily the controls moved. The only other transport category airplane I had flown was the DC-3. The flight controls on that airplane were manual, with cables going directly from the yoke to the ailerons, rudders and elevators, and they were fairly stiff. The C-141 had hydraulic boosted controls and it was like the difference between cars that have power steering and those that don't. It was easy to fly.

We flew around for four hours that day and it felt like two. We went round and round the pattern. Once in a while one of us would take a coffee or bathroom break. I could not believe how relaxed it all was.

The next day we found ourselves back to the flight simulator. We spent the next twenty hours of training in there. That was not fun, but it was the best place to be exposed to all the emergencies we might encounter in the airplane. Here we learned how to handle those emergencies in a safe environment.

We flew nine more flights in the airplane with George Mizell, and then it was time for our Second Pilot Checks. I took mine with Captain Norm Janes. Everything went well and I was finished with C-141 Initial Training. I would receive more training once I got to Charleston, but most of it would be on-the-job during my MAC Missions.

George invited me over to his home for a farewell dinner. I got to meet his beautiful wife Barbara. She fed us a delicious steak dinner and we had a very pleasant evening together. I really enjoyed my time with George Mizell. He was so much fun to fly with.

As I was leaving he said, "Good luck in the 76th Squadron Mike. That's a damn fine outfit, and they are getting a damn good pilot in you. I hope we run across each other again some day."

"Thank you, George, I hope so too. Flying with you has been a blast!

I suddenly realized that my logbook was going to be filling up fast at this rate. I was knocking on the door of my first 1,000 hours of flying time!

It was now time to go check into the 76th Military Airlift Squadron, which was a part of the 437Th Military Airlift Wing. I had chosen Charleston because I wanted a base where a lot of my trips would be to Europe, and, because I grew up in the south, I believed I would feel at home there.

When I checked in at the 76th Military Airlift Squadron I received a nice warm welcome. I was given a schedule and told to go to base housing to set up my living arrangements. I decided to stay at the Visiting Officer's Quarters until I finished orientation. While I was there I met Travis Scott, another new member of the 76th. He was also a bachelor officer.

Travis and I went through orientation together and we hit it off pretty well. The folks at Base Housing told us we would probably have to get an apartment off base because the BOQ was full. We would get an extra housing allowance for that. We decided to go in together and find a place to share. That way we could afford a nicer place. We got lucky and found a great apartment located right on the edge of a beautiful swamp. The apartment was just fifteen minutes from the base. We got a nice two-bedroom place and after we moved in, we discovered there was a mix of people living there from the military and civilian life. Most of them were young like us.

Not long after I joined the 76th Military Airlift Squadron, we had a squadron party at the officer's club. There were a lot of new Lieutenants in the squadron and I think they wanted to introduce us to the rest of the pilots and their wives.

The party was nice and I got to meet a lot of people. I didn't know at the time that these squadron get-togethers were rare. At any one time about one third of the squadron pilots would be out on the road. The war was raging and we were going to be flying our butts off supporting it.

Charleston Air Force base was a joint military and civilian facility. It was a huge airport in terms of facilities and not so large in terms of runways. There were just two runways available. One ran in a north / south direction and the other in a northeast / southwest direction. The second runway was the shorter of the two.

The Air Base was located on the western side of the runways, and a civilian terminal and control tower were on the eastern side. There was a fair amount of civilian airline traffic in and out of the airport, but it never seemed to interfere with our Air Force Operations.

From what I can recall, the 437th Military Airlift Wing consisted of two C-141 Squadrons. They were the 41st and the 76th. It was an amazing sight to see dozens of shiny new C-141's parked wingtip to wingtip on that ramp. We were still getting new airplanes straight from the Lockheed factory the entire time I was in Charleston. There is nothing like taking a brand new multi-million dollar airplane out on a trip. It beats that new car smell by a mile.

There was an Air Defense Command squadron of F-101

"Voodoo" Aircraft based there too. The Commander of that squadron lived near me in the apartment complex. I begged him to take me on a ride in one of his fighters. He said he would, but he never did.

Travis Scott and I were taken up on a local training flight and we were all given our second pilot check rides. There was a low overcast when we took off that morning and we flew several approaches in and out of the clouds. We would take off and enter the overcast at around three hundred feet. We flew the entire traffic pattern and approach in clouds, and we broke out at three hundred feet. Sometimes we would continue and make a touch and go landing, and other times we would make a missed approach. We had to be proficient in both of those things. This was my first experience in actual instrument meteorological conditions. Instrument flying with this kind of equipment is a piece of cake.

Chapter 7

Flying the MAC Line

I flew forty-eight trips while I was based in Charleston, because I was young, single and eager to get out there and learn some things and see the world. I also wanted to log the required flight time to upgrade to Aircraft Commander as soon as possible so I volunteered for extra flying. Consequently my life in Charleston, for at least the first year, consisted of flying five to seven day trips, coming home for a few days, and going out and doing the same thing again often to the same places. Most of the trips were routine, some were very exciting, and some were filled with surprises.

So, come along with me and see what life was like for a young bachelor pilot flying in the Military Airlift Command during 1967 and 68.

Mike in the left seat of the C-141!

Flight Log: February 20, 1967
Aircraft Commander – Lieutenant Colonel William Harris

My phone rang at 0400. It was the Squadron alerting me for my trip. When they scheduled me for this trip I was told to pack enough clothes for five to seven days. That meant three flight suits and a set of civilian clothes for layovers. I had to be at Squadron Operations at 0500 for preflight planning.

Flight planning for a trip like this was quite involved. The Navigators did the actual route planning, but the Aircraft Commander had to monitor and approve everything involved. The Flight Engineers checked in with us, and then they went out to the airplane to do the preflight inspections. There was another Copilot assigned to this trip. He was a Major, but I can't recall his name. Colonel Harris was a nice guy, but he was a straight arrow, meaning I had better be a straight arrow too, at least during this trip.

The first leg was a short one. We had to stop in Dover AFB, Delaware to pick up our cargo. We took off into cloudy skies and never really broke out. We entered the clouds at three hundred feet and exited them again at three hundred feet on approach in Dover. It was like sitting in the Flight Simulator for a couple of hours.

After picking up our load we departed for Anchorage, Alaska. Out total time from Charleston to Dover to Elmendorf AFB, Alaska was ten hours and twenty minutes. About six hours into the trip my butt started getting numb.

In 1967 there was a steady stream of C-141's flying into Vietnam and other bases in Southeast Asia. To keep the cargo moving, the Military Airlift Command (MAC) devised a system of Staging Crews at outlying bases. For example, when our airplane landed at Elmendorf, there was a crew waiting to take it on to Yokota AFB in Japan. Our crew would Remain Over Night (RON) at Elmendorf and pick up another C-141 when it came through. We sometimes had to wait as much as forty-eight hours for our next flight. We usually had some idea of how long it would be and we planned our layover activities accordingly. The more time we had, the more things we were able to do. We staged at all the bases throughout Southeast Asia.

Elmendorf was a great place to be. I fell in love with the State of Alaska right away. It was so wild, clean and beautiful. Of course it was cold as hell but we were prepared for it. We had a separate flight bag full of winter flying gear just for Alaska.

The Officer's Club was the only place to go up there, and it was not far from the Visiting Officer's Quarters where we stayed. I remember the Stag Bar special was a hamburger steak, and it was delicious.

On our first RON I ran into a familiar face. It was Colonel Wahl, who was the T-38 Squadron Commander at Webb when I went through that program. I don't remember what his job was at Elmendorf, but he was way up on the wing staff. He remembered me too. We sat and talked quite a while.

"Mike, we IP's were all surprised when you chose a C-141 over a fighter assignment. We all agreed that you were a natural fighter pilot and we thought that was what you would do. I also considered inviting you to come back to my squadron as a T-37 instructor. With your previous civilian experience and your UPT performance, I felt you would have been an excellent instructor."

I explained some of my reasons for not taking a fighter assignment, but at the end of the conversation I said, "But Colonel Wahl, I messed up on my choice and I know it now."

I visited with Colonel Wahl several times over the course of the next two years. Every time we got together he would give me some treat to take home. It might be smoked salmon one time and moose meat the next. He was a genuinely nice guy.

On day two we flew to Yokota AFB just outside Tokyo, Japan. I remember a funny incident that happened while we were eating breakfast. I was sitting at the table with Colonel Harris and the Major when one of our flight engineers came up to us to tell us that the airplane was ready to go. Then he turned to me and said, "Lieutenant Trahan, I have a bet with the other enlisted men. I told them you were a Coonass. Was I right? Are you a Coonass?"

"Yes I am Sergeant and I'm damn proud of it!"

I thought the two officers with me were going to fall out of their chairs. The Major said, "I can't believe you are going to sit there and let an enlisted man call you a name like that and not do anything about it."

"No Major, what he said was not an insult to me." Then he gave me the setup I was waiting for.

"Well then, what is a Coonass anyway?"

"Major, you mean you don't know what a Coonass is?"
He said "No."

"A Coonass is a little hole under a coon's tail!"

We all had a good laugh, at his expense, and then I explained that Coonass was slang for Cajun. The sergeant had recognized my Cajun name.

After breakfast, we did our flight planning and went out to the airplane. This was my overwater check out and it was very interesting.

The sky was clear and the visibility a hundred miles when we left Elmendorf and headed west. I was awestruck by the beauty of western Alaska and the mountain range we were flying over. It all just looked so CLEAN! We saw several inactive volcanoes on our way out to the Aleutian Chain. Once we departed the Aleutian Islands we didn't see land again until we coasted out in Japan.

I crossed the International Dateline for the first time on this trip. I believe we flew into tomorrow on our westbound legs and back into yesterday on our eastbound legs. I don't really recall now, but it took a little getting used to. The navigators notified me when we crossed. I asked if there was some kind of initiation or celebration for this and they said no. They did say that there was an initiation and celebration for crossing the Equator.

I remember watching the Navigators as we crossed the North Pacific. We were close to the Russian border, and we definitely did not want to get too close. The Cold War was still raging and we would have been in big trouble had we violated their airspace. In fact, not too many years later a Korean 747 blundered into the Russian airspace not far from where we were, and the Russians shot them down – passengers and all! The Navs were very alert and diligent until that danger passed. Our time from Elmendorf to Yokota was eight hours.

I did not get to do much flying on this trip. I was there mostly to observe how it was done. I had only two duties to perform. I was responsible for carrying and keeping up with the Secret Codes we were required to carry on all our missions. If we got an in-flight change in mission orders, we had to authenticate the change using the codes. My other duty was to monitor the High Frequency Radio when we were out of VHF radio range. Other than that, I just sat on the jump seat and watched. Yes, it got very boring at times.

There was one great thing about Yokota Air Base Officer's Club. Yokota was probably the busiest hub in the entire Far East and almost everyone going east or west went through there. The all wound up at the O' Club. Consequently, you never knew whom you might run into there. During the time I was flying through there I ran into quite a few people I knew. The specialty at the Club was the "Sizzerin" steak sandwich and YOC French Onion soup. It was a combination that could not be beat.

There was a little village called Fussa City, which was located just outside the gates of the base. Fussa City was where a lot of the MAC crews went for a "Hotsie Bath" and a Massage. I didn't go this time, in deference to Colonel Harris, but I did make it over there on subsequent trips.

I vividly remember our housing arrangements at Yokota. A great number of MAC trips went through Yokota on their way to Vietnam and other SEA bases. Consequently, housing was at a premium. Our entire officer crew slept in one big common room that had at least ten beds in it. Sometimes members of other crews slept in there with us. It was hard to get uninterrupted sleep in that situation.

The first night I was lying in my bunk, not more than five feet from the bunk being occupied by a Lieutenant Colonel. I asked, "Colonel, is this what I have to look forward to when I have twenty years in the Air Force like you do?"

"Yep Lieutenant, I'm afraid it is!" That was not encouraging.

On February 23, 1967, I made my first trip into Vietnam. I was surprised and pleased when Colonel Harris invited me to take the right seat on this leg to Danang.

There were two approaches into Danang Air Base. The most desirable was to land to the south because you were over water until you were on short final. Landing to the north meant flying low over some rice paddies and there was always the threat of taking ground fire from that area. We landed to the north this time. Danang Control Tower warned us that we could expect ground fire on short final. Sure enough we got some! At first I wanted to hunker down behind the instrument panel, but I realized that was stupid. I couldn't land the airplane that way, and besides, if they were going to hit me then there was not a lot I could do about it anyway.

After landing we discovered there were several bullet holes in the belly of the airplane. Once the mechanics determined that nothing vital was hit, they just patched up the holes (with super duct tape) and we were all set to go again.

Danang was a fascinating base. It was one of the largest bases in Vietnam and it was busy! It was our closest base to North Vietnam, and a lot of missions over Hanoi and Haiphong were launched from there. There were all kinds of aircraft flying out of Danang. I saw at least two squadrons of F-4's and one B-57 squadron. I also saw some AC-47 "Spooky" Gunships on the ramp. I had heard about that airplane. It was known as "Puff The Magic Dragon" and it flew night close air support missions for troops in contact. I wondered what that mission was like.

C-141 aircraft rarely spent the night in Vietnam, so after unloading our cargo in Danang, we took off for Kadena AFB in Okinawa. The flight time from Yokota to Danang to Kadena was nine hours.

Kadena was one of the nicest places we stayed over there. Okinawa was owned by Japan and it was just like being in Japan. The specialty there was Kobe Beef Steak. That was, without a doubt, the best steak in the world. They also served Mongolian Barbeque.

Kadena was also one of those huge multi-command bases. The most exotic airplane that flew out of Kadena was the SR-71 Blackbird. We only got to see it take off one time, but it was spectacular.

I ran into my UPT Classmate Dick Lyle at Kadena on this trip. He was flying the KC-135 tanker aircraft out of there. Dick was there on a Temporary Duty Assignment, aka TDY. His squadron was based at Fairchild AFB in California. They were on a six-month rotation supporting the SR-71 mission as well as the Vietnam mission. The tankers would orbit off the coast of North Vietnam and wait for fighters to come off their targets. The fighters pretty much stayed in full afterburner while over North Vietnam, so they were hurting for fuel when they came out of there. Dick and I had a nice time catching up with each other.

We spent just one day in Kadena and were soon on our way back to Elmendorf. Nine hours later we were there!

On February 25, 1967, we departed Elmendorf for the "Lower forty-eight states", and we landed at Andrews AFB. We left the airplane there and hitched a ride to Charleston on an old C-124 Globemaster.

The trip home on that old antique airplane took forever

it seemed. But it was the only opportunity I had in my Air Force Career to fly in that old bird. We were gone just five days on this trip. This turned out to be the average length trip we flew, and I usually got two or three of them a month.

There was a nice incentive for us to fly into the active war zone. For every month we flew in the Saigon Flight Identification Region (FIR) we were awarded combat pay and we got a five hundred dollar income tax deduction. After all, when we were flying in and out of there we were just as exposed as aircraft based in country. Hell, we took some hits on this first mission! That sounds like combat to me.

I came home from this trip with mixed emotions. I was excited about flying this magnificent airplane all over the world, and this first trip was a great adventure. However, I realized pretty quickly that I had gotten used to one hour and thirty minute flights in Pilot Training, and these legs were usually eight hours or more. I knew about four hours into that first leg that I may have screwed up. I thought about what life would have been like in fighters. Their flights were usually no more than an hour and a half at a time! The average MAC flight was eight hours or more. It was going to take me awhile to get used to those long haul flights but they were also the kind of flights that would fill a young pilot's logbooks!

Had I made a big mistake in choosing transports when I could have had a lot more exciting and wild ride in fighters? I may have, but there was no turning back now. In this Air Force once you were classified as a Multi-engine pilot you pretty much stayed there! The chance of ever having another opportunity to fly fighters was very remote.

I put those thoughts out of my mind and I looked at the

bright side. I was in for a lot of travel and adventure in this new job of mine, and I was getting experience in a Transport Category Jet Aircraft. Money could not buy that kind of training. I decided to stop looking back and wondering what if?

I noticed that the Aircraft Commander and the First Pilot (Copilot) took turns flying the airplane from the left seat. The AC usually started out in the left seat, but on each subsequent leg, he and the copilot would change seats. I liked that. It gave the copilot experience in the Aircraft Commander's seat where he would eventually be. I asked Colonel Harris how long it took to make Aircraft Commander in the 76th Squadron,

"Our wing requires 2000 hours of total Air Force time before you can check out as AC. At the rate we are flying right now that will take you about two years to achieve. Unfortunately, we are so fat on AC's that we have the luxury of giving our copilots more experience before checking them out. It helps our safety record, but it's not a good deal for guys like you who are chomping at the bit to be in command of your own aircraft. The 437th Wing is the only one in MAC that requires 2000 hours. The rest of them will check you out in 1500 hours."

Well folks, there you have it! I didn't want to fly F-4's because I didn't want to be a damn copilot, and here I had sentenced myself to at least two years in the copilot seat of the C-141. To me that sounded like a little overkill in on the job training, but I decided I would pay attention and learn everything I could during those copilot years, so when my turn came, I would be ready.

Flight Log: February 28, 1967

"All Weather Landing System" Checkout
Instructor Pilot - Captain Larry Tuzzo.

As I look back on this, I am a little amazed at how advanced the technology was on the C-141. It was way ahead of the times in Transport Category Aircraft Technology. This airplane had what was known as an All Weather Landing System on it. The autopilot was so good that you could couple it up on an Instrument Landing System (ILS) approach, and it would fly the airplane all the way down to and through touchdown! It was the first Auto-Land system I would encounter.

I had to be checked out on this system before they could send me out as a fully functioning copilot. We flew a local flight to Warner Robbins, GA and shot ILS approaches there.

I realized something else about this MAC life I had chosen. I had just put the screws to my social life! I saw how the schedules were running for the copilots and it appeared we would be making at least three trips per month with each of them being five to seven days in duration. That meant our off time at home would come in three or four day spurts, and we never knew when that would be. Consequently we could not make plans for being home for anything. It was just the luck of the draw, and we new copilots usually got the short straw in all the drawings. They flew our young butts off, and that was just fine with us.

With an erratic schedule like this, if I did meet a girl, I would have to find one who understood and accepted that kind of uncertainty. We may be able to go out three nights in a row, or we may go weeks without seeing each other.

Someone willing to put up with that was hard to find.

There were a few single girls in the apartment complex. The first one I met was Delores "Dody" Wallace. Dody lived a couple of doors down from Travis and me. She was a teacher, but she had recently been a Delta Flight Attendant. The one time I asked her out she turned me down. She was upfront with me about it.

"Mike, it just does not pay to date someone who lives close to you. If it works out between you two fine, but if not, it could be hell. I had an ex-boyfriend living near me one time and after we broke up, he gave me fits. He was always sticking his nose in my business. So, can we please just be friends? We can do fun things together but we can't get serious."

"Of course we can Dody. I am an expert at being just friends. But, this means you are going to have to fix me up with some of your Stewardess Friends!" She just laughed.

Jim Carr and his wife set me up with a Catholic nurse. Her name was Katy. Katy and I hit it off right away. We looked like we might be headed somewhere, until Sheila Niedzwiecki re-entered my life!

Travis and I had not seen much of each other. It seemed that when I was out he was in and vice versa. It was months before our schedules meshed again. However, that was not all bad. It was kind of nice having that apartment all to myself once in a while, and I'm sure Travis felt the same way.

Flight Log: March 4, 1967
Aircraft Commander: - Major John Wright.

After four days in Charleston, including a local flight, I

was back on the road again. My first trip was strictly an observation ride, but this time I was working for my flight pay. John flew the first leg from Charleston to Elmendorf.

On March 5, I flew the leg from Elmendorf to Yokota, Japan. This was my first time in the left seat on a line trip, and it felt great. It was also the first time I had flown the C-141 at its maximum gross weight of three hundred sixteen thousand and five hundred pounds. It felt solid as a rock. The 141, when light, tended to bounce around a lot. At these weights it just sliced through the air and responded so smoothly to my control inputs. Our time en-route to Japan was ten hours.

On March 7 we flew from Yokota to Bangkok, Thailand. Time en-route was seven hours twenty minutes. This was my first time in Thailand and I found Bangkok a fascinating city. We were housed in a nice hotel downtown, so we had an opportunity to look around quite a bit. We took a great tour of the city and saw the Floating Market and The Reclining Buda. In fact, we visited several Buddhist Temples. The food was delicious too.

Another thing I noticed in Bangkok was that the women were beautiful and exotic looking. Apparently they appreciated the presence of Westerners because most of them made an effort to learn the English language.

On March 9 we flew from Bangkok to Tan Son Nhut AFB, in Saigon. It was just a short hour and a half trip. This was my first trip into the capital of South Vietnam. We departed Tan Son Nhut a couple of hours later and flew to Yokota.

My UPT roommate, Jim Roberts, was based at Tan Son Nhut at that time. He went straight from UPT to the War Zone in C-123 aircraft. I didn't get to see him this trip, but I did on subsequent trips.

On March 11 we flew an Air Evacuation flight from Yokota to Elmendorf. The airplane was converted to a flying hospital with nurses traveling with the wounded. It was a terrible scene. There were probably sixty litter patients and another forty wounded men sitting in some airliner type seats that were set up for them. I was very impressed with the Flight Nurses. They were dedicated people. Fortunately we had some great tailwinds that trip and we made it to Alaska in just under seven hours.

There was one funny moment in this otherwise very sad and depressing flight. As we approached Elmendorf the head Flight Nurse made a public address announcement. I guess she was practicing for a Flight Attendant job later on.

"We have enjoyed serving you on this flight. We hope you have the opportunity to fly Air Evac with us again sometime!"

"Er, I don't think so!" I thought.

I noticed something on this trip. We seemed to be spending an inordinate amount of time flying at night. I don't know why that was, but I soon understood why some people called MAC the Midnight Air Command. Our motto was, "Sun down – landing gear up! Sun up – landing gear down!"

I was not scheduled to fly again in the near future. I was told to just go home, relax and the Squadron would call me when they needed me. So, I did just that.

This time off gave Travis and me a good chance to get our apartment set up nicely and to get to know each other a little better. Travis was a very quiet guy and he did not divulge much about himself. I knew he went to flight school at Moody AFB in Valdosta, Georgia and that he was in 67C at that base too. His hometown was Montgomery Alabama.

We each had some stereo components so we combined what we had to create a nice system. We even had a turntable and a tape player. I believe we went together and bought a television for the living room.

Dody Wallace came over one day for a visit. She asked, "Mike, would you like to take me out Friday night?" I said an enthusiastic yes, and I asked her if she had changed her not dating a neighbor policy for me.

"No, this isn't a date. I want you to take me to see James Brown and the Famous Flames. He is playing in Charleston and I am afraid to go by myself. We will probably be the only white people there."

"Well okay Dody I'll go, but it will have to be Dutch treat. No loving no paying!"

"I knew you would say that. I already have the tickets. I am treating you this time."

Flight Log: March 23, 1967
Tactical Airlift Training.
Instructor Pilot - Captain Bill Thalberg

Tactical flying included flying formation and dropping parachute troops or cargo. We learned how to "station keep" using our radar to hold position on the lead aircraft, and we also practiced fingertip formation. It was pretty exciting getting wingtip to wingtip with another giant airplane. It was a very interesting mission. I was now a "TAC" First Pilot.

Flight Log: March 29, 1967
Aircraft Commander - Major Blank

I had been warned about Major Blank. He was known as a "strictly-by-the-book" kind of guy, but that was not a problem for me. I actually preferred pilots who did it by the book, up to a point.

On March 29 Major Blank flew us to Elmendorf. We had to wait two days for our next airplane to come through the stage.

On March 31 I flew the leg to Yokota, Japan. It must have been a routine crossing because I made no notes in my logbook.

On April 1 we flew to Tan San Nhut AB in Saigon. We offloaded our cargo and were back on the road to Kadena, Okinawa in just a couple of hours. They didn't like keeping the C-141's loitering on the ramp in Vietnam for long. Any base over there was vulnerable to rocket or mortar attack at any time.

On April 3 we took off from Kadena to Elmendorf. I was in the left seat and Major Blank was sleeping in one of the crew bunks. The flight was going well until we were almost half way from Kadena to Elmendorf in terms of time. This was known as the Equal Time Point or ETP. Then we lost an engine!

We were five minutes short of the ETP when we had to shut down the #4 engine. We had low oil pressure and high oil temperature on that engine and the emergency procedure said to shut it down. I should have waited to wake Major Blank and tell him about the engine, or we should have lied and told him we had already reached ETP because the first question out of his mouth was, "Have we reached ETP yet?" And stupidly we said no. His automatic response to that was, "Okay then, we have to go back to Japan!"

We told him the weather in Japan was bad and getting worse but it was clear and a million in Alaska. We also said the winds had picked up over the North Pacific Route and we were going to be tight on fuel getting back to Yokota when it would be a breeze getting into Anchorage. He would have nothing of it. He insisted we return to Japan. Like I said, he was a by the book kind of guy. The book said if you had not reached ETP you turned back. This night the book overrode common sense and it got us in a lot of trouble.

We called Air Traffic Control and declared an emergency, so we could reverse course and head back to Japan. We requested Yokota as our new destination and we were told that the Yokota weather was getting worse. It was already three hundred feet overcast with blowing snow. Winds were gusting to fifty miles per hour. It was not looking good for a landing at Yokota. We were given Itazuke AFB as an alternate just in case we needed it.

Sure enough, when we were approaching Yokota, we learned that the field was closed because of blizzard conditions. There was a whiteout down there and the winds had increased to seventy mph. We continued to Itazuke, which was a considerable distance west of Yokota. The weather there was not that great either, but we managed to get in. We notified maintenance and they checked the engine out. It was a faulty oil pump. So this entire exercise was a waste of time and money. We spent the night in Itazuke.

On April 4 we flew directly from Itazuke to Elmendorf.

The tailwinds, which were headwinds for us the night we diverted to Itazuke, were nearly 200 mph. We made it to Alaska in seven hours twenty minutes.

On April 5 we flew from Elmendorf to Dover AFB, Delaware. We spent the night in Dover.

I had just flown my third MAC trip, and it was already starting to feel like I was doing the same thing over and over. I really didn't expect it would be like this. I thought, by flying out of Charleston, I would be going eastbound to Europe at least half the time. But then, I didn't realize the major impact the Vietnam War would have on our missions. The war WAS our mission during those years.

Flying through all those times zones took a toll on my diurnal cycle. My body didn't know if it was midnight or noon most of the time. After I got home, it usually took me a day or two to get my body acclimated back to the Eastern Time Zone. Most of the time I would barely have time to do that before it was time to go out again. This was one of those times. I had three days off. My next trip was scheduled for April 10! This kind of flying was a young man's game. I didn't know how those "old" forty five year old Colonels were doing it.

Flight Log: April 10, 1967
Aircraft Commander - Major Dick Glogowski

Richard M "Dick" Glowgoski was one of the "Good" guys. He was definitely not a typical major. Being an Air Force Major was kind of awkward. Majors were above the Lieutenants and Captains, so they didn't hang out with us, but they didn't fit in with the Lieutenant Colonels and above either. All of them were striving to make Lieutenant Colonel! Consequently, more than a few of them were a little ruthless in their dealings with the junior officers around them, and they did whatever would make them look good, so they could reach that next rank. If that meant stepping on a few junior officers' toes – so be it!

We lowly Lieutenants had a running joke about Majors: "What does the Air Force and the Ancient Greeks have in common?" Answer – "They like to hide their pricks under Oak Leaves!" The symbol for the rank of Major was a golden oak leaf.

Dick was none of those things. In fact, he was just the opposite. I thoroughly enjoyed flying with him, and apparently he enjoyed my company as well because shortly after that trip he hired me to work in his office as my Extra Duty. He was in charge of Training for the 76th Squadron, and we kept up with all the training records and requirements for the squadron. I was gung ho to fly a lot, but later on, it was nice to take a week a month and work in the office instead.

On April 10 we departed Charleston for Kelly AFB in San Antonio where I had gone in the summer of 1965 to take my Air Force Qualification Physical.

I remembered the emotions I felt that day, and how relieved I was to know I was finally going to get into the Air Force. Kelly is a pretty large logistics base and we were there to pick up some important equipment to take to Vietnam. It was wrapped and marked Top Secret, so I never knew what it was. We stayed at Kelly overnight and departed for Elmendorf AFB the next morning. We spent twenty-four hours at Elmendorf and headed for Yokota on April 12.

After we landed and checked into the BOQ at Yokota, we all jumped into the bus and rode over to Tachikawa AFB about twenty miles away. "Tachi" had a huge Base Exchange and they were having a great sale on Sansui 5000A Stereo Receivers. We were all into the best stereo equipment we could find back then, so we wanted to take advantage of the sale. We were still in our flight suits!

When I walked into the entrance of the BX, I noticed a staircase to my left. Something caught my eye at the top of the stairs and I stopped and looked up. Standing there was one of the most beautiful women I had ever seen. She was carrying shoeboxes under each arm. When she looked down and saw me standing there she exclaimed, "Mike Trahan!" and she dropped the shoes. She ran down the stairs, threw her arms around my neck and gave me a big kiss right on the mouth. I could not believe my good fortune!

I leaned back, to get a better look at her, and she said, "You don't know who I am do you?" I told her to just keep doing what she was doing and it would eventually come to me. She said, "You big jerk, I'm Jo Cormier. You took me to the Homecoming Dance your senior year!" Jo was from West Orange, Texas. She was two years behind me in high school there.

I hugged her closer. "What are you doing here in Japan Jo?"

My imagination swirled. *"I am a single lady just waiting for someone like you to come into my life."*

The bubble burst when she pushed me back a little bit and said, "I am here with my 6'4" tall, karate - knowing, Air Force Academy - graduate, Lawyer - Husband!"

"Well let's go meet him!" And we did. Forty years after

this happened I saw Jo again, and neither of us had forgotten it. It was just one of those little fun surprises that life gives you from time to time.

On April 13 we flew from Yokota, to Danang, and then to Kadena. I think this was the trip where we went downtown and got Kobe Beef. I have never had a better steak in my life! Afterward, we took a little tour of the town, and parts of it were really sleazy.

On April 14 we flew back to Elmendorf. On this leg the weather in Anchorage was quite a challenge when we got there. We didn't have enough fuel to go anywhere else, and the weather was right at minimums for approach. This was my first approach down to 200' ceiling and ½ mile visibility, and it was quite interesting. In order to get in, we had to fly a coupled approach and use the auto-land system. It was nice to see the system working for real.

On our final leg home we made a stop in Dover, Delaware, and after a short stop in Dover we headed home to Charleston.

I had only flown four trips and had already picked up over 200 hours of flying time. At this rate, I was going to reach my two thousand hours in no time.

I had two weeks off after this trip. I had to sit down because I had most likely exceeded my monthly 125 hours of flying time. I am a little hazy on this, but I believe we were allowed to fly 125 hours a month, 300 hours a quarter, or 1000 hours a year.

Sheila Niedzwiecki and I had been corresponding regularly and I told her about my promotion. She sent me a card. "Congratulations on your First Lieutenancy!" I didn't even know there was such a word as Lieutenancy, and

I kind of teased her for using it but had to apologize later because she was grammatically correct.

Sheila also said she had bid for and had gotten an assignment to fly Braniff MAC Supplemental Charters on the East Coast. She would be flying as far north as Gander, Newfoundland; Halifax, Nova Scotia; Goose Bay, Labrador; and Thule, Greenland and as far south as the Panama Canal and Ramey AFB Puerto Rico. Her layover bases were going to be Dover AFB, Delaware and Charleston AFB, South Carolina. I told her I was delighted to hear that, and I hoped she and I would get to spend some time together when she was in Charleston. She said she hoped so too! She said she would start flying the MAC Charters in July and I would see her then.

Flight Log: May 5, 1967
Aircraft Commander – Lieutenant Colonel Bill Harris

Although my fifth MAC trip was routine, we had a problem on the leg from Yokota to Kadena. The copilot's windshield started arcing, and we had to have the window heat element replaced in Okinawa.

Then, on the layover in Kadena, I was awakened in the middle of the night by a strange noise. I could not identify it because I had never heard it before. I opened my eyes and felt the bed shaking, and then I saw my night stand moving across the room. I had just experienced my first earthquake. It was probably around a 3.0 on the Richter scale and it was very unsettling!

Flight Log: May 13, 1967

Aircraft Commander - Captain "Moose" Miller

We departed Charleston on May 13 and flew to Kellogg Field in Battle Creek, Michigan. We were there to upload cargo, but most importantly, it was a nostalgic trip for Captain Miller, since Battle Creek was his hometown. We didn't have time to do anything there, but Moose was happy that he got to fly this big ole airplane into his hometown airport.

We departed Battle Creek and flew to McChord AFB in Tacoma, Washington, picked up some more cargo at McChord, and flew on to Elmendorf.

The rest of the trip took us to Yokota; Clark AFB in the Philippines; Bangkok, Thailand; Yokota; Elmendorf; and Dover AFB.

This was my first trip into Clark. It was a giant base and a major hub of travel to and from the war zone. Every time I passed through there I ran into someone I knew. One time I ran into Gene and Kay Gunn who had been at Webb when I was there. Gene graduated a few months before I did.

I also ran into Major Gene Taft, my Flight Commander when I was in T-37. He was now Flight Commander of an F-4 unit there at Clark. His unit rotated in and out of Vietnam on a TDY basis. I learned later that Gene had shot down a North Vietnamese Mig 21 on one of his missions over there.

Flight Log: May 23, 1967
Aircraft Commander - Major John Casada

This trip was an interesting one because it hardly involved any flying. We took an empty C-141 to Pope AFB near Fort Bragg in North Carolina and just parked it there. The

Army wanted to ship some Huey Helicopters in the C-141 and they had to figure out the exact ramp angle in order to get that bird in the cargo area. We spent five days at Pope while they worked on their project.

On the fifth day the Army finally figured out how to load their helicopters in our airplane, and we were free to go home.

Major Casada was one of the good guys, and I had a lot of fun with his last name. I used the long letter "a" and it sounded like I was saying Caaaasssssaaaaada.

"Mike! You are putting the emphaaaaasis on the wrong syllaaaaaabbbbussss!" He would then pronounce it the correct, shorter way.

My next trip didn't involve flying, but I was sent to Pope AFB again. The 76th Squadron was providing some C-141's for parachute practice for the 82nd Airborne Division and they needed an Air Force Drop Zone Safety Officer on the ground during these drops. That way, if something went wrong there would be someone on the ground to document it from that angle. I was chosen to be DZ Safety Officer that week.

One day we were out there and the commander of the 82nd Airborne Division, a Two Star General invited me to ride in his jeep. We were sitting there watching string after string of jumpers pouring out of the C-141's flying overhead. Each airplane dropped about 90 jumpers.

Everything was going fine until the fourth airplane came over the jump zone. It dropped its load and about halfway into the string of parachutes, we noticed one guy dropping at about twice the normal rate. He had a malfunction and he was too low to cut away from his main chute and deploy his reserve. He hit the ground like a ton of bricks! We sped over to where he landed, and the General jumped out and walked over to him. The guy was lying flat on his back and the General said, "Airborne!"

The poor soldier jumped up, saluted, and said, "All the way Sir!" Then he fell back down. He was okay, just a little shaken up. The General congratulated him on his good technique in landing.

"Good PLF Son (Parachute Landing Fall). Your training saved your ass today." It was an interesting insight into Army life for me.

That was the last drop of the day, and I was glad of it. The General looked at me.

"Mike, you look a little shook up. Let's go to the O'Club and I'll buy you a drink!" Those Army guys were pretty surprised to see an Air Force First Lieutenant sitting at the General's table!

Flight Log: June 7, 1967
Aircraft Commander - Capt. Bob Johnson

My eighth MAC trip was my first time into Travis AFB just outside San Francisco. It was beautiful, and after landing there I kind of wished I had requested to be based there.

On this trip, the navigator was listening to the ADF Radio, which picked up the local radio stations. As we were on approach to Travis he said, "Hey Mike, listen up on ADF #1." I pulled up the monitor switch and heard the song, "If you're going to San Francisco, be sure to wear some flowers in your hair!" Why that has stuck with me all these years is a mystery to me.

I mentioned the "Hotsie Baths" earlier in this story, and that was one of the first things I learned about when I got to the squadron. I had not had the opportunity to go see what they were all about until this trip.

When we landed at Yokota, Bob and the Navigators decided they wanted to go over to Fussa City just outside the base gates and get a massage. They invited me to come along. Now bear in mind that this massage parlor was not what you usually envision when someone mentions massage parlors. This one was legitimate, meaning no "hanky-panky." It was so legitimate that the wives of the officers stationed at Yokota went there for massages too.

I will have to say that this was one of the most pleasant experiences of my entire MAC career. When you have flown for eight or ten hours there is nothing better than a nice steam, a hot rinse, and a wonderful massage to fix you right back up.

I had seven days off this time, and after months of "severe drought conditions" my social life took off. I think I had a different date just about every night I was home. I met girls left and right, but Katy Coyle was my favorite, and we had hit it off very well. She was the only Catholic girl I was dating, so that may have had something to do with it.

Dee Keyser called me up. Jerry was on a trip and she needed an escort to some Squadron function because they lived about twenty miles from the base and Dee didn't want to drive home alone late at night. I said I would be happy to go with her. It wasn't a date, but it was a very pleasant evening with a very beautiful and very sweet lady. At the end of the evening Dee told me she had a girl she wanted me to meet the next time I was off.

Flight Log: June 26, 1967
Aircraft Commander – Major Dean Caseleman

I had a brief visit with my Air Force Pilot Training room-mate Jim Roberts at Tan San Nhut Air Base on this trip. It was just a lucky encounter that we saw each other at base operations while we were flight planning our next flight.

Jim said he was living off base, in an apartment down-town. He said the place was a madhouse with humanity piled on top of humanity, but he liked it. I voiced concern for his security and he just brushed it off. He said, "Nothing happens in downtown Saigon!" He would have to eat those words a few months later when the Tet Offensive hit that town. I wished him luck and we were on our way.

After this trip I had some time off and, I don't know what I was thinking, but I agreed to do something that was pretty dumb. Some officers in our squadron challenged some en-listed men to a flag football game. They knew I played some at Ole Miss and asked me to join them. I did.

It was a good thing I had a date with Katy Coyle that night, because she was a nurse, and after that game I needed a nurse! About halfway through the game I jumped over someone lying on the ground and I hyper-extended my right knee. I knew immediately that I was done for the rest of the game. By the time we got home my knee had swollen to twice its normal size. Katy iced it down for me. I spent the rest of my time off getting back in shape for my next trip. However, I didn't report the injury to the flight surgeon. I found I could walk okay a couple of days after the injury so I felt confident I could make a trip. That was a big mistake. My leg hurt like hell on that trip.

Flight Log: July 6, 1967
Aircraft Commander – Captain Glen Simpler

MAC Trip Number Ten finally took me to Europe. I had bid to fly out of Charleston because I had always wanted to do some flying around Europe. It took me about seven months, but this trip was a dream come true.

We departed Charleston on July 5 and flew nonstop to Torrejon AFB in Madrid, Spain where we had a RON. Captain Simpler introduced us to Roast Suckling Pig at "La Casa Botine" in downtown Madrid. I've never tasted anything better.

We also went to the bullfights, although I didn't care much for them. One thing I noticed was that all the men in downtown Madrid wore suits. That came as a surprise, and it made us Air Force guys stand out like a sore thumb. I also noticed how beautiful the Spanish women were.

On July 6 we flew from Torrejon to Goose Bay, Labrador, where we spent the night. It was my first trip near the Arctic Circle.

On the way into Goose Bay we heard one of the funniest exchanges I have ever heard on air-to-air radio communications. There is a reporting point in Labrador called Mon Joli and it is pronounced in the French dialect. An airplane called in, "Mount Jolly Radio, this is Pan Am 566 at Flight Leven 350."

The controller came back, "Pan Am 566, this is MON JOLI

Radio", and he said it with the strongest of French pronunciations for emphasis.

The Pan Am pilot came back, and in perfect French, he gave his position. Mon Joli Radio came back and said, "Er, Pam Am, we don't speak French down here."

Pan replied, "Very well, as I was saying, MOUNT JOLLY Radio, Pam Am 566...."

Chapter 8

My Life is About to Change --- Drastically!

Sheila Niedzwiecki

Sheila Niedzwiecki was now flying the Atlantic MAC Trips she bid for. She had five days off between trips, so we decided she would spend some time in Charleston with me. We had four great days together.

Being together felt different to both of us this time. Up to now, I had known her only as Allen Natella's girlfriend, and I always kept a respectable distance from her. However, during that time we had developed a very nice friendship. It was a bit of an awkward transition from being friends to dating each other. In fact, at one point I said, "Sheila, is this a date, or are we still hanging out as friends like we did in Big Spring? I just want to be sure I know what the ground rules are."

She answered, "Yes, we are now officially dating!" And then she smiled a mischievous smile. I got the feeling she knew something I didn't, and as it turned out later on, she did!

Our time spent talking, touring Charleston, and hanging out together gave us a great opportunity to get to know each other better and to decide if we wanted to pursue this relationship any further. It turns out we did.

Flight Log: July 12, 1967
Aircraft Commander – Colonel Dunlap

This was my first trip into Cubi Point Navy Base. It is a tight approach and the airport is surrounded on three sides by mountains. The only way in or out was over the water. I came in high and blew the approach. I just could not safely get the airplane down to landing position in time. The Navy controller sent me around by saying, "MAC, take a wave-off!" Fortunately we Air Force types knew a wave-off meant to go around!

I flew over the runway and did a 360 degree overhead pattern, using forty-five degrees of bank. This was the type of approach they taught us in TAC Training, but people seldom saw a C-141 make that kind of approach. Those were reserved for the fighters. The Navy guys were impressed, and so were Colonel Dunlap and the rest of the crew. The rest of this trip was routine.

Flight Log: July 19, 1967
Aircraft Commander – Captain Ray Lotts

This was a short trip up to Thule, Greenland. It was the farthest north I had ever landed. We made a stop in Dover on the way up.

The navigators told me that we were so close to the Magnetic North Pole that standard navigation was unreliable. They used what they called Grid Navigation. They tried to explain it to me but it was too complex for me to understand.

We spent the night in Thule and departed the next day for Charleston with a stop at Andrews AFB.

Sheila and I had spent a lot of time writing letters and talking with each other on the phone. I just sensed she was going to be the one for me. So, I decided to stop going out with other women and explained to them I felt I had found the "one".

Flight Log: July 27, 1967
Aircraft Commander – Lieutenant Colonel Leroy Ohrt

This was my first trip into Denver since the adventures in my Cessna 140 back in 1965. This time I had plenty of power to takeoff and climb out! I shared that little story with the crew when we left Denver.

After this trip, I took a week of leave to go to West Orange for a visit with Mom and Dad. It had been several months since I had seen them, and I invited Sheila to come down too. I felt it was time for my parents to meet her and vice versa.

I picked a great time to be home on leave. This was purely by accident, but my friend Florence "Flo" Rhodriguez was getting married to Roy Housewright that weekend. My parents, Sheila and I went to her wedding together on August 5.

The next day my friend Larry David and I took Sheila and his date water skiing in Cow Bayou. Sheila was not too crazy about the murky water of the bayou. She preferred to be able to see what was in the water with her, but she got in the water anyway. I gave her big points for her bravery.

When we got home from skiing I parked in the driveway behind the house. Dad was sitting in his favorite spot on the back porch, and when Sheila stepped out of the car in her red bikini bathing suit, I could see him raising the window next to him. I knew he was going to say something completely inappropriate to embarrass her, and he didn't disappoint me.

With a whistle he said, "Wow, what I wouldn't do with something like that!" Dad loved to intimidate people with outrageous comments.

Well he picked the wrong person to intimidate this time. Sheila walked straight into the house and in her wet bathing suit, she sat right on Dad's lap and said, "Okay big boy. What would you do?"

Dad got all flustered and said, "Aww, go take a bath!" Sheila had his number from that day forward.

It was during this visit that Sheila and I both realized that we had something very special together. We had not dated that much, but we had known each other a year-and-a-half and had spent a lot of time together when I was in Big Spring. I decided start concentrating on our relationship. I'm glad I did. We were not quite ready to declare to each other that we were in love but both of us knew we were.

When she left to go back to Dallas, she promised to come see me in Charleston as soon as possible.

Flight Log: August 12, 1967
Aircraft Commander – Captain Bill Thalberg

MAC Trip #14 is memorable for its in-flight emergency. On August 19 we departed from Elmendorf to Charleston. At Rotate Speed I noticed my airspeed tape going to full scale high and the Aircraft Commander's going back to zero. We obviously were losing our airspeed indicators. We declared an emergency and Bill Thalberg flew the airplane by using attitude and power settings to keep us out of trouble. We had no idea how fast or slow we were going. We suspected there was something wrong with the central air data computer and there was no way to fix it in flight. We had to return to Elmendorf for maintenance. Unfortunately for us, the weather was overcast, and penetrating those clouds without airspeed indicators would have been very dangerous.

About that time another C-141 came up on frequency. He knew about our problem. He and Bill decided we would fly on their wing and make the approach. They would take us down until we saw the runway, and then they would go around and we would land. Bill did an excellent job, and we landed without incident.

We could not have asked for a better pilot for this particular emergency. Bill Thalberg was an excellent pilot, as well as the Squadron expert on Tactical Formation Flying. He did a magnificent job holding position with the lead airplane. Our view of the other airplane was minimal in those thick clouds, but by holding perfect fingertip position we

Mike Trahan

never lost sight of him. Bill even let me fly formation a little from the right seat.

We were told that Pan American Airways was doing some filming at Elmendorf that day and they got a film of us coming in on the wing of that other airplane. I never got to see the film though. I wonder if it still exists?

After we landed we found out that someone had re-moved the drain plugs on the pitot system causing the CADC (Central Air Data Computer) to malfunction. These two things were what produced reliable airspeed indications on our instrument panels. Investigators later determined it was sabotage. The mechanics were able to fix the airplane in a couple of hours and we were on our way to Charleston.

When we arrived at Charleston the weather was right at minimums. They were reporting ceiling one hundred feet and visibility one and an eight of a mile, with ground fog. We used auto land and barely got in. I was glad we did, because I had company waiting for me back at my apartment. Sheila Niedzwiecki had come for another visit.

It was on this visit that Sheila and I finally talked about our future together. We had both been single long enough and we were both ready to settle down. We spent four won-derful days together enjoying each other's company and get-ting to know each other on a completely different level. On the last night of her visit, I got a call from Crew Scheduling assigning me to a local flight at 0600 the next morning.

I was not expecting this flight. Sheila was visiting me and we were having a great time. I thought scheduling was going to leave me alone, but they needed a Copilot to play student for Bill Wirant who was getting his Instructor Pilot rating. I was the only copilot available. I didn't want to be there, and it showed.

Flight Log: August 23
Instructor Pilot - Bill Wirant
Check Pilot - Colonel Mike Messenger.

I flew a lousy flight. I apologized to Bill afterward and told him I just mentally wasn't there. He laughed, "Actually Mike, it worked out great. You gave me a lot of things to comment on and correct!"

When I got back home I showered and shaved. I took Sheila to lunch and then drove her out to the airport for her flight back home. When she left I felt very good about our future together. She did too.

Flight Log: August 24, 1967
Aircraft Commander – Major Fred Wackym

My strongest recollection about MAC Trip 15 was how pleasant it was to fly with Fred Wackym. For a Major, he was exceptionally nice. When we got back to Charleston Fred recommended me for my First Pilot Training and Check Ride. He said I was ready.

I was starting to get to know more of my neighbors at the apartment. Our immediate next-door neighbors were Charley and Jackie Hyatt. They had a lovely little girl who was about two years old. Her name was Christen. Charlie was in the Navy. He was seldom around, but Jackie and I had developed a comfortable friendship.

When Sheila left after her last visit I went over and

talked with Jackie.

"Jackie, I think she is the one I'm going to marry." That was the first time I had expressed that possibility to anyone. I hadn't even said anything to Travis about it. Jackie had met her and she approved of my choice.

"She is a lovely and sweet girl Mike, and I can tell she loves you by the way she acts around you. I think you are making a wise choice."

Flight Log: September 3, 1967
Instructor Pilot - Major Fred Wackym.

It was time for me to check out as First Pilot on the C-141. Right now I don't even remember the difference between Second Pilot and First Pilot. Fred took me out and gave me a good workout. He recommended me for my First Pilot check the next day.

Flight Log: September 5, 1967
Flight Examiner: Colonel Walterhouse.

First Pilot Check ride passed. It was a good ride. Colonel Walterhouse was impressed with the way I kept up my publications and the way I organized my flight kit.

I had quite a bit of time off between trips, so I took some leave time. When Sheila visited me in August she invited me to come to Dallas to meet her parents. I had met them during one of my visits to her apartment with Allen Natella, but this time she was introducing ME as her boyfriend.

When she picked me up at the airport, I knew the decision I made before leaving Charleston was the right one. I had already decided to propose to her! I planned to wait until we were in some romantic setting to pop the question, but as soon as I saw her I could not restrain myself any longer. I asked her to marry me right then and there in the airport parking lot. She said yes!

I kind of had a feeling Sheila had some news for me, so I asked, "Will this be a long or short engagement?"

She laughed, "A short one Mike. We are going to have a baby in about eight months!"

We were both fine with the fact that a baby was on the way, because we had already decided we wanted to settle down together. I took this as a sign that God had chosen Sheila for me, and I was very happy with His choice.

No, it was not the ideal situation, but we felt we could work through any problems, which might come up. It's now forty-eight years later and we are still happily married, so I guess it worked out okay.

I recalled the days I was back at Webb AFB, and Sheila was there, visiting my classmate Allen Natella, who was introducing her to all of his classmates. Her beauty, especially her gorgeous eyes, had struck me the moment I met her. As I walked away I thought - I hope I find me a girl like her some day. I had no way of knowing it then, but I had just done that!

I asked Sheila how we came about, and she really surprised me with her answer.

"Mike, I had a feeling about you the moment we met. When you asked me how to spell my name that feeling was validated, and when you remembered how to spell it two weeks later, that pretty much solidified it. I knew within weeks after we met that you were the man I wanted to marry!"

I was flabbergasted.

"What about Natella? You sure seemed to be pretty serious with him?"

"Allen was just a guy to have fun with, Mike. I knew you were nowhere near ready to settle down, so I had fun with him."

"Then what about your setting me up with your roommate Donna? That got pretty serious too."

"I introduced you to her so I could keep an eye on you, and, like I said, I knew you weren't ready to settle down."

"When you broke up with Donna, and I caught Allen cheating on me that opened the door for us."

"But that happened seven months before we finally got together. Why did you wait so long to make your move?"

"Because I knew you had been working on your flying ratings since you were fifteen years old, and you had sacrificed a lot of your social life in the process. I knew, once you got your Air Force wings and had accomplished everything you wanted to, you would want to explore the world a little bit and sow a few wild oats. I waited until I felt you had all that out of your system and you were ready to settle down. Then I bid the Atlantic MAC trips and came to Charleston to be with you!"

"Sheila, from the way you describe it, my fate was sealed a few weeks after we met!"

She kissed me and said, "Yes it was!"

We went to her parent's house and visited with her father Stan and her mother Winnie. We told them that we wanted to get married in October, but we didn't tell them they were going to be grandparents. They were delighted and welcomed me with open arms. I met Sheila's only sibling on this visit. His name was Jerry Don, and he was a couple of years younger than her.

Sheila was not Catholic, so I knew we would have to see a Priest and get her some instructions in order for us to get married in the church. Fortunately we were able to get an appointment the next day. Father talked with us both and we explained the situation to him. He got me alone and said, "Are you doing this under your free will or under duress?"

"Father, I love Sheila and I want to marry her pregnant or not. This is definitely not a shotgun wedding."

"Well, I had to ask!"

He told Sheila she would have to come in a few times to learn what was expected of a Protestant mother of the children of a Catholic man. Sheila was fine with all of the requirements because she was familiar with the Catholic Church. Her father was Polish, and his entire family, except him, was Catholic. He was baptized Catholic, but he had married a divorced woman, so he could no longer practice that faith. Anyway, we got all those details settled in record time. We even went to town and bought matching gold bands for our wedding.

I spent a couple of days there with them, and then I flew down to West Orange to see Mom and Dad. I told them that Sheila and I had decided to get married in October, and I also told them that they were going to be grandparents. Dad was okay, but I think Mom was pretty shook up by the news. I told her how I felt about Sheila and after that, she was fine with it. I said we were going to be married at Saint Michael's Church in Farmer's Branch on October 21. I asked Mother to go to St Mary's and get copies of my Church Records to send to the priest at St Michaels. She said she would.

I had to find a best man, and the first person to come to mind was my old roommate Don Walker. Don was with the Peace Corps in Africa, so he was not available. I asked Jerry Davis to stand with me as best man. Sheila asked Neta Dial to be her maid of honor. With pretty much everything settled, I flew back to Charleston.

Flight Log: October 11, 1967
Aircraft Commander – Major Bobby Johnson

I left on this trip with great concern that I would not get back in time for my wedding. When we got to Kadena they wanted to send my crew back for another trip into Vietnam or Thailand. That would have made this trip at least two days longer. That would have kept me out dangerously close to my wedding date of October 21. I was able to swap with another copilot who was on his way home, so I got home in time to make it. I wish I could remember the name of the copilot who swapped with me.

When I got back to Charleston I sat down with Travis Scott and told him that Sheila and I were engaged and would be getting married shortly. I said I would have to move out and get an apartment for Sheila and me, and I would have to do it pretty quickly. Travis said he understood, and then he surprised me by saying, "Mike, I've seen this coming since the first time Sheila came here. You two are perfect for each other! I am very happy for you." I apologized for moving out on him so suddenly.

"Think nothing of it Mike. I think I will enjoy having the place all to myself for awhile."

I went to the leasing office and told them I was getting

married. I asked if they had any apartments available. They said they had a one bedroom we could move into right away. I said that would do for a while, but that we would need a two bedroom in about seven months. They put us on a wait list for the first two-bedroom unit that came up, and it was not long before we got a good one.

Chapter 9

Sheila Niedzwiecki and I Get Married!

I flew to Dallas on October 19 because I wanted to save some leave time, and since our wedding was very simple there were no more arrangements to be made. Sheila had taken care of all of them. The wedding date was October 21, 1967.

It was an interesting coincidence that Sheila and I were getting married exactly three hundred and sixty-five days after my graduation from Undergraduate Pilot Training. I like to tell her now I had just one year of freedom and carefree living!

Mom and Dad drove up from home on the 20th. That

night Dad treated us to a Rehearsal Dinner. It was a very intimate, nice dinner with my parents, Sheila's parents, her brother Jerry Don, along with Neta Dial and Jerry and Judy Davis.

The wedding took place the next morning at ten o'clock. My grandfather Adolph Trahan and my Uncle Donald and Aunt Willie Blanchard, and their son Richard attended with us. Larry David was there too. In fact, Larry took the only pictures we have of the wedding.

On Sheila's side of the aisle there were a lot of people from San Angelo. They were Winnie's family, the Corbells. They were from an old West Texas ranching dynasty and they were characters! Her maternal grandmother, Bertha Corbell, was there. When I was in Dallas to tell her parents we were getting married we also told Bertha. Her response – "I knew it was going to rain today!"

We didn't have a Mass. I guess because Sheila was Protestant at the time. That was a disappointment to me. We didn't wear traditional wedding clothes either. Sheila wore a beautiful tan dress and I wore my blue suit. I guess I should have worn my Air Force Uniform, but it didn't occur to me. Our wedding was about as simple and low key as any I have ever attended. It lasted about five minutes total.

After the ceremony we went to Sheila's parent's home for an informal reception, which included a Wedding Cake and a foot tub full of iced down beer.

After the reception, Jerry Davis drove us to the airport and Sheila and I took a Delta flight back to Atlanta at four pm. The Orange contingent of the wedding party saw us off at the airport and then they went to the Texas State Fair for a while.

We decided to spend two nights in Atlanta before going

on to Charleston. It was not much of a honeymoon, but it was better than nothing. We went to see the movie "Bonnie and Clyde" our second night there. We stayed in the NEW Holiday Inn at Atlanta Airport both nights. That hotel was to become a major part of my life later on because I would be spending a lot of layovers and training days there. But that was a few years down the road.

We flew on to Charleston on October 23. Sheila liked the new apartment. We only had a couple of days to settle in before I went out on another trip. Fortunately Sheila had met some of the people in the apartment complex during her visits with me, so she was not left there completely alone in a strange place. She drove me to the Base for my trip, so she would have some transportation while I was gone.

I left on this trip a little concerned about Sheila. She had undergone such a major transition in her life in such a short period of time. A month ago she was flying around the world for Braniff and now she was grounded, married, pregnant, and sitting in a one-bedroom apartment all alone for however long I would be gone. I prayed she would be okay.

Flight Log: October 26, 1967
Aircraft Commander – Dean Cassleman

At long last, I drew another trip that didn't go west to the War Zone. This trip was truly interesting because we went to some very exotic places I had dreamed about all my life. I'd read about Brazil, Ascension Island, Kinshasa, and Addis Ababa in my geography books and found them fascinating. Now I was going to get to visit them.

Our first leg took us to Patrick AFB in Florida. Patrick is

adjacent to the Kennedy Space Center and that is where NASA stages supplies and equipment for their tracking stations down range. We were there to pick up some of that equipment.

After a short stop at Patrick we left for Recife, Brazil. Recife is on the easternmost point of Brazil about halfway down that country. Unfortunately, most of our flight over South America was in darkness. We got to keep our airplane all the way around on this trip, and that was nice!

We ran into another MAC crew at the layover hotel in Recife. We didn't have time to go exploring on this layover but they told us a little about the place. The most interesting to me was their description of the local House of Ill Repute! It was a building on the shoreline. Because it was so close to the water it was built up on tall pilings. Consequently, it was known throughout the MAC world as the HOS or House on Stilts!

The next day we headed across the Atlantic Ocean. This was my first Atlantic crossing and we crossed at probably the widest part there is. We had to stop at Ascension Island to drop off some NASA parts. There is a NASA tracking station on Ascension.

The one thing I remember most about that place was the wonderful cafeteria where we ate. I believe it belonged to NASA. I think they compensated the workmen who were isolated on this island in the middle of the south Atlantic with great food.

After a two-hour stop at Ascension, we headed to Africa. Our total flying time was only seven hours twenty minutes. We must have had some pretty strong tailwinds on that leg.

Kinshasa is the capital of The Congo, or at least it was

back in 1967. Its former name was Leopoldville. The President of the Congo had two American airplanes at his disposal: a C-47 and a C-123. Our government provided two American Air Force pilots to fly them. One of those pilots was Major Douglas Gipson and I didn't get the name of the other one. Staying downtown was unsafe for our crew, so we were boarded at the home of these two pilots. They lived in a huge mansion overlooking the Congo River. The view was spectacular!

My diurnal system was messed up by jet lag, so I woke up in the middle of the night. I decided to step out on the beautiful veranda and enjoy the moonlit view of the Congo River, which was less than a half-mile away down the hill. There was a full moon that night.

I was enjoying this wonderful scenery when I heard a rustling noise in the bushes surrounding the veranda. I looked down and saw a short native in a loincloth, with his bow and arrow pointed at me. The arrow was drawn back to fire. I yelled for Major Gipson and he came running out there.

"Mike, that's my guard. It's a good thing you didn't turn and run into the house. We would be plucking a poisoned arrow out of your ass right now if you had."

"Well, thanks a lot for letting us know he was here."

Gipson laughed, "And spoil the surprise?"

Then he and his "guard" started laughing. It was a damn setup!

The next day Dean and I went downtown to look around. Major Gipson told us to be very careful and stay on the major streets. He said to avoid alleys because there was a good chance if we went into one we would not come out.

I was running low on cash, so I told Dean I wanted to go by the US Embassy, which was just a block away to cash a check. I could see the Embassy from where we were standing. Dean said he had plenty of cash and would spot me whatever I needed. So we didn't go to the embassy. And what a shame that was!

Two weeks after I got home from this trip I got a letter from the US Embassy in Kinshasa. It was from Lorraine Forbes, the girl I dated during both of my years at Ole Miss. Lorraine was writing to tell me that she and Major Doug Gipson were engaged. She was working in the very same embassy that I didn't go into that day. What a shock it would have been to both of us to run into each other in the middle of the Congo.

On our third day in Kinshasa we did a turnaround to Addis Ababa, Ethiopia. That trip took us all the way across the Congo and it was quite a treat. Addis is 9500 feet above sea level, making it one of the highest elevation airports in the world. We were pretty heavy when we landed, because we still had plenty of fuel left. We came very close to running off the end of the runway before we stopped. Our nose was sticking over the end when we turned off.

We only stayed an hour. Then we turned around and flew back to Kinshasa. This time, because we still had so much fuel, we elected to fly low level so we could enjoy the view. We cruised across the Congo at two thousand feet and two hundred and fifty knots. We could see animals everywhere. We even saw Mount Kilimanjaro in the distance. I'll never forget that flight.

The next day we flew back to Ascension and Recife. We had a little bit of a problem getting away from Kinshasa though. When we got there the night before they parked us up close to the terminal. When we got ready to push back the tug would not start. Dean elected to BACK out of there using engine reverse. That was a little dicey.

We picked up a load of workmen at Ascension. They were going to Recife for a week of Rest and Relaxation. I flew this leg and when we landed at Recife I kind of plopped it on the runway. It was not my best landing. The Loadmaster opened the door so I could hear the passengers booing me.

I got on the public address mike, "Screw you guys! Loadmaster, secure the cabin for takeoff. We are going back to Ascension, unless I see a big attitude change back there."

We spent the night in Recife and then headed home to Charleston. It was one of the most interesting trips I had in the C-141. In fact, it was one of the most interesting trips I've had in any airplane.

I asked Sheila how she fared while I was gone. She said she did fine. She went to the base, bought some groceries, and explored it some. She also visited some of our neighbors and they welcomed her with open arms.

We decided to go to Charleston and buy a bedroom set. We found a beautiful king sized Mediterranean set which we both liked. It was made of solid oak and it was beautiful. Link Taylor made it and it was called Majorca. We also bought a Motorola colored TV.

When it came time to leave the store I asked how much they wanted down and they said nothing.

"Well, I will start paying on it now. How much is layaway each month?

The guy laughed, "Haven't you ever bought anything on credit?"

I looked at Sheila and she shook her head no. I turned back to the guy and said, "No, I guess we haven't." He told us we could make a note and they would deliver the furniture to us that very day! We were so surprised.

Sheila and I both paid cash for everything we bought and we took it home when it was paid for. That's the way we were raised. We still have that bedroom set and it is still as good as it was the day we bought it, forty-eight years ago.

We went to some formal Squadron function not long after we were married. I was so proud to have my beautiful wife on my arm that night.

Flight Log: November 8, 1967
Aircraft Commander – Capt. Dean Heal

MAC Trip 18 was what was known as a "Junction Run." On this run we hit some pretty major capitals. It appears we flew these to establish and keep our air routes to these places active and open.

One memorable thing about this trip was landing in Adana, Turkey on a major Muslim holiday. Nothing was open on the base except the cafeteria, not even the library. We had absolutely nothing to do for the three days we were there. I did a lot of walking around and thinking. I was still getting used to the idea that I was a married man with a child on the way, and the responsibility was weighing a little heavy on my heart that trip. I also did a lot of praying on that trip.

We then spent a night in Frankfurt. This was the first time in my life I experienced Déjà vu! We were walking in downtown Frankfurt when someone said they were hungry. I said, "When we reach this corner we will be on Kaiser Strasse. There will be a bunch of hookers on one side of the street and a bunch of restaurants on the other side. We can get something to eat at a beer garden that's about halfway down the block." I have no idea where all that came from, but it was exactly as I described it.

Flight Log: November 23, 1967
Aircraft Commander - Major Don Casteel

This would have been a wonderful trip at any other time, but at this time it was not a good deal. My new bride had planned a nice Thanksgiving Dinner and had invited a couple of bachelor officers to join us, including Ray Caracci-olo.

I got a call from scheduling two days before Thanksgiving saying I had a trip to Rio de Janerio. It was just a flight down there, spend the night, and fly back home. I would be going over Thanksgiving. Sheila was not real happy about that, but I had little choice in the matter. I asked them if there wasn't a bachelor pilot who couldn't have taken the trip and they said nobody was available but me.

I thought to myself, *"Well Ray Caracciolo is available. He is coming to my house for dinner!"*

We got down to Rio in time to go out for the evening. We stayed at the Regente Hotel on Copa Cabana Beach. Needless to say, the mini bikini clad ladies on the beach were spectacular.

That evening we went downtown and had a great meal for hardly any money at all. I remember all kinds of meat, warmed at your table over an open flame, and cut right there for you. We even had time to take a tram up to Sugarloaf Mountain. Rio, at that time, was a beautiful and clean town. It was pretty safe to move around down there. Sadly that is not the case these days.

We headed back to Charleston the next day. It was a short trip, and I enjoyed flying with Don Casteel.

Flight Log: November 28, 1967
Aircraft Commander - Major Don Casteel

The only thing noteworthy about MAC Trip #21 was my chance encounter with Sheila's old boyfriend Allen Natalla. I ran into him at the Yokota Officers Club the evening we arrived there. He had flown up from Ubon, Thailand where he was a member of the famous "Triple-Nickel" Squadron.

News travels fast when airplanes are zipping around the world at .80 Mach, so I did not get to break the news to Allen that Sheila and I had gotten married. Someone else beat me to it. Al was pretty shocked because he didn't even know that Sheila and I had dated. I think he was a little upset too.

I told him that Sheila and I had seen each other in Dallas when I was on my way to Tinker. I said that was after he and she broke up. I told him she and I had stayed in touch, and we started dating six months later.

"Allen, I never even came close to making a pass at Sheila when she was dating you, but after you two broke up, I felt like she was fair game." He seemed okay with that. But frankly, I didn't give a damn whether he was okay with it or not.

I noticed Allen had some "nervous ticks" when we talked. I was not sure why he was reacting like that, but after he started telling me about his missions over North Vietnam I understood. He was suffering from combat fatigue, or maybe PTSD.

His squadron, the 555th or "Triple Nickel" was one of the most famous in the Air Force and they were an aggressive outfit. I can imagine being a GIB in one of their F-4's was pretty intense. GIB means "Guy in the back Seat" on the F-4. That was the lousy job pilots got right out of UPT.

Sheila and I had been married just fifty-five days and I had already flown six trips and I had been gone thirty-three days. That kind of schedule can make adjusting to a new marriage difficult. We were still feeling our way around this marriage thing and getting to know one another.

We spent a lot of time driving around Charleston and

going out to the barrier islands off the coast. They were very peaceful. We even went to a party or two at the apartment complex.

Flight Log: December 16, 1967
Aircraft Commander - Captain Dick Chapin

This was just another routine PACAF trip. They were all starting to feel the same to me, and that was not a good thing. I thought all this traveling around the world would be educational, and it was to some extent, but I didn't get to spend nearly as much time in these exotic places as I would have liked. We usually had only enough layover time to get a good meal and eight hours of sleep before it was time to go again. All the airports were starting to look the same too. That fighter slot I passed up was starting to look better and better.

We had some leave time, but it was so close to Christmas we decided to stay in Charleston rather than try to fly to Texas during that busy time. We went to a Christmas party at Craig and Tudie Morrison's house on Christmas Day. It was nice being with the other married couples. This was Sheila's first time with most of them.

On December 26, Sheila and I flew to Dallas. We wanted to pick up her Ford Falcon and drive it back to Charleston. She needed some transportation while I was on trips. It was also getting hard for her to get up at 0400 to take me to work.

We spent a couple of days in Dallas with Sheila's parents. We told them Sheila was expecting a baby and it would be born sometime in May. They were excited to have a grandchild on the way. Sheila's brother Jerry came by once or twice. I think he was working for American Airlines, on the ramp, at that time.

We got Sheila's Falcon and drove down to West Orange for a visit with my parents. It actually felt a little strange sleeping with my new bride in the same bedroom that had been mine alone for so long.

Dressed up for the DERA Dance

This was a nice visit though. I took Sheila around and introduced her to more members of my family, and we went to the DuPont Employee's Recreational Area (DERA) Club House for a New Years Eve Dance.

On our drive back to Charleston we stopped for a visit with Glen and Jan Doss in Florida. He was based at Tyndall Air Force Base near Panama City.

Glen had arranged for a T-33 when he learned I was coming to visit. I had my flight suit and boots with me. The plan was to fly a local and then go out and do some aerobatics, which I had not done since I left pilot training. Alas, it was not to be.

When we got to the base Glen discovered there was a travel pod attached to the belly of the airplane we were going to fly. We went into Base Operations and they told Glen they needed him to fly a part to Andrews for another airplane that was broke down there. So, that's what we did. I was so disappointed that we didn't get a chance to go out and flop around in the sky, but it was nice to have a ride with Glen in his airplane. I had never flown in a T-33 before, and as it turned out, this was the only time.

When we got to our cruising altitude Glen gave me control of the airplane. I could not hold the damn wings level. The T-33 had a little quirk. It has very strong aileron boost and there is a little slack in the stick where neutral aileron is. Someone who flies the airplane regularly can handle that quite well, but anyone new to the airplane, and especially someone who has been flying transport aircraft, would have a problem with it. I also could not read the 1950's style instruments he had in there. After fighting it for a few minutes I said, "Screw it Glen, you fly it!"

I got so tickled at him during the ride up there. He was very quiet, as one who mostly flew solo would be, but once in awhile he would say, "Oh shit!"

"What is the 'Oh shit' about Glen?"

"Dropped my pencil."

A little while later, he said "Oh shit!"

"What's up Glen?"

"Dropped my map."

Just as we were starting our descent into Andrews he

said it one more time, and in the same tone of voice, "Oh shit!"

I asked him what was wrong and he said, "We're getting a little low on oil pressure."

"Glen, isn't this a single engine airplane?"

He said it was indeed a single engine airplane.

"Well, I really think your last "Oh shit" should have had a little more emphasis than the first two. Losing oil pressure can lead to engine failure and since we only have one that would be a real OH SHIT in my book!" We both laughed.

It was bone chilling cold when we parked on the ramp at Andrews. I was practically hypothermic by the time we got out of the airplane. In fact, a crew chief had to come help me out. It was very cramped back there.

While they were servicing the airplane and loading the part Glen and I had a cup of coffee in Base Ops. The mechanics checked the oil system and everything was okay. Glen said, "It's a good thing we didn't have to bail out today. As big as you are Mike, you probably would have been banged up getting out of that little cockpit. "

We had an uneventful flight back to Tyndall. As we started our descent, Glen did a victory roll for me. I entered this flight in my logbook when we landed. I wish I had gotten him to sign it for me.

After our visit with Glen and Jan, we drove on to Charleston. It was a nice leave. But now it was time to get back to work.

Chapter 10

My Last Year in the C-141

Flight Log: January 13, 1968
Aircraft Commander - Jim Caldwell
Navigator - Charley Funk

One thing I particularly remember about MAC Trip #23 was running into my 67C classmate, George D'Angelo, at Cam Ranh Bay. George was flying F-4s out of there. Our visit was interrupted by a mission briefing he had to attend. He invited me to come along so I did. We sat in the back of the room and the Squadron Commander announced that they were going to start bombing in North Vietnam again. There was an audible groan throughout the room. Flying up North was dangerous stuff.

I told George that Sheila and I had gotten married, and, of course, he already knew. Like I've said before, news travels fast in the world of jet aviation. I wished George good luck and told him I would keep him in my prayers. I'm happy to report that he made it home just fine, and he went on to have a distinguished Air Force career.

Flight Log: January 26, 1968   "Embassy Run"
AC Col Weyhrich
FP Major Howerton
FP Mike Trahan.

The Embassy Run was a desirable trip because it was so unique. We took off from Charleston, headed east, and circled the globe from East to West. We kept the same airplane throughout the trip, and it was a high priority Department Of Defense mission, which meant that we were first in line for support anywhere we went. Another advantage of keeping the airplane was that we could pretty much haul anything we wanted to back home. A lot of guys bought Hibachi Pots, which were big clay barbeque pits. We also all bought some ornate wooden screens in India. The cargo bay was full of that stuff by the time we got back.

I had never been to Pakistan, India, Guam or Hawaii, so this was a very interesting trip for getting to new places. We laid over in Madrid, New Delhi, The Philippines, Guam and Hawaii.

It was near midnight on January 30 when we landed at Tan San Nhut AB in Saigon. Midnight marked the beginning of the Vietnamese New Year, or Tet, as they called it. We knew about the holiday, and we saw all kinds of flares, rockets, and tracers being shot up into the air. We actually thought this was all part of the celebration.

When we contacted Tan San Nhut tower we were told differently. They said, "MAC, we are under attack down here. We want you to land, drop your cargo on the taxiway as you taxi back to take off, and then get the hell out of here. We recommend you have at least three thousand feet of altitude by the time you reach the perimeter of the base! Watch out for ground fire. A lot of it has been reported on approach too."

We did exactly as they said. After landing we rolled

down the taxiway dropping our cargo. Fortunately everything was on pallets and nothing was damaged in the process. When we got back to the departure end of the runway we immediately took off. We overheated two of our four engines as we climbed out at maximum power and pitch to get above three thousand feet and out of small arms range. Fortunately, we had enough on board that we didn't have to land anywhere else in Vietnam for fuel that night. Every base in that country was under attack that night. We had stumbled into one of the most famous events of the entire war – the beginning of the 1968 Tet Offensive!

We flew back to Clark AFB, and then on to Guam, Hawaii, Travis AFB, and home.

When you fly completely around the world in five and a half days, it takes a toll on your body. I was totally exhausted after this trip. I barely had enough time to recover before it was time to hit the road again.

I felt bad for Sheila. She was starting to look a little bewildered by my crazy schedule. I imagine she was having a few second thoughts about that time. I don't think this was the ideal family life she envisioned when she dreamed of married life.

Flight Log: February 5, 1968
Aircraft Commander - Major X.
Navigator - Warren Martin.

When I reported to the squadron for this trip, Larry Tuzzo called me aside.

"Mike, the AC you are flying with is a little weak and

prone to make mistakes. Keep a close eye on him!"

"Well hell Larry, why don't you put me in the left seat and let him keep and eye on me?"

"You are one of our strongest copilots Mike. We are going to put you in AC training as soon as possible. In the meantime, help us out by keeping these weak AC's out of trouble. Can you do that for me?" I said I could.

As it turned out, flying with the best and the worst Aircraft Commanders in the squadron was a great education for me. When I flew with the best I learned what to do, and when I flew with the worst, I learned what not to do.

This was my first trip into Korea. Kunsan was like the face of the Moon. It was one of the most barren, ugly places I have ever seen. We didn't stay long thank goodness. We offloaded and refueled and flew on to Korat, Thailand.

On departure out of Kunsan, we were assigned an initial altitude of 10,000 feet. Major X was flying and he was climbing at a very high rate as we went through 9,000. I alerted him that we were only cleared to 10,000 and he overshot by about fifteen hundred feet. Just as we leveled off and were going back down through 10,500 we HEARD a C-130 cross right above us. He was at 11,000'. We were damn lucky we didn't have a mid-air collision that day. This was what Larry Tuzzo was warning me about. You just never knew when Major X would have a brain fart and do something stupid like that.

During our stop in Korat, I ran into Major Larry Kleinstiver. Larry was in charge of Aviation Physiology at Webb when I went through there. He was flying F-105's out of Korat. He was about to go home though. He ripped his right hand and damaged some nerves when he reached into his map case for a map. He caught a piece of jagged metal. I believe he was almost finished with his 100 Missions anyway.

Fighter pilots who flew into North Vietnam were so exposed to being shot down and or captured that the Air Force thought it was only fair to them that they would have to fly a certain number of missions over there. Then they could go home. They came up with the number 100. In World War II the odds were so bad for surviving a mission the magic number was just 20 missions.

I just had three days off after this trip, and I felt my schedule was starting to get a little ridiculous. I wondered where the hell all the other pilots were. How could it be that I was the only copilot available for these trips? This time Sheila expressed her exasperation with this crazy schedule.

Domestic Trip - Flight Log: February 23,24,25, 27
Aircraft Commander – Capt Joe Bammert

Captain Bammert and I flew this same trip four days this week. I believe Crew Scheduling took notice of how much I was gone from home and had some compassion for Sheila and me. They assigned me to some domestic flying over the next few days.

This series of trips was quite different from anything I had flown so far in MAC. In fact, they more resembled a domestic airline day than a military day. We flew a round robin trip to several bases on the east coast. I believe we were carrying NORS parts to these different places. NORS meant "Not On Ready Status" and the parts we carried were what was needed to put the airplane back in commission. It was actually a pretty important mission. The best thing about flying the Shuttle was that I was HOME every night.

Sheila and I were able to take advantage of these days off because I was not all tired out and messed up from crossing time zones. In fact, we stayed in the same time zone the entire week. It was fun mixing it up with the airliners that were flying up and down the east coast. Our flying days were comparable, but the pay was definitely not.

We were really enjoying the stability of my being home for some weeks at a time. We even made plans with friends. One night we went to dinner with the Sellmers and the Morrisons. That was so pleasant.

One day we got a call from the Apartment Leasing Office. A two-bedroom apartment had become available. It was on the bottom floor on the corner of the same building we were in. We went down and took a look at it and we liked it. We asked if we could move in right away and they said we could. They said they would just take what we paid in rent for the one bedroom we were in and apply it to what we would owe for the bigger place.

I called Travis Scott and a couple of other guys there at the apartment and we were moved into the new apartment in just a couple of hours. Of course, now we were obligated to feed Travis and the other two guys who helped us. So we did.

The doctor said our baby would arrive sometime in early May. Sheila and I started looking for furniture for the other bedroom, which would become the nursery. We found a crib and had it all set up in no time.

Sheila and I had thoroughly enjoyed my time at home this past month. I came in from my last Pacific trip on February 19 and here it was March 15 before I had to go out again. It was also time we needed to get things ready for our baby.

Flight Log: March 15, 1968
Aircraft Commander – Capt. Harry Bennett

Harry Bennett was one of my favorite Aircraft Commanders. He was just a really good-natured guy and a pleasure to be around. Sometime during my tour at Charleston, Harry was promoted to Major. I flew with him shortly thereafter and said, "Well Harry, it's been nice knowing you but I guess I can't be your buddy any more." I told him the joke about the Military and the Ancient Greeks hiding their pricks under oak leaves. He laughed and said, "Mike, you will be a Captain soon, and the difference in our ranks will be the same. So, don't worry about anything changing between us, because it won't. And it didn't. Harry was that kind of guy.

With a baby on the way, I felt that we needed a more reasonable family car. I discussed it with Sheila and she agreed it might be easier to have a car that wasn't a stick shift. I went to town and traded the GTO in on an Oldsmobile Cutlass. I think I got screwed in what they paid me for the GTO. It was a 1965 model, with a 389 cubic inch engine, three two barrel carburetors, and a four speed manual transmission. That car sells for over $100,000.00 today! I think I got $1500 for mine.

I was happy with the Cutlass, but I wondered how I did in my first new car negotiation. I doubt that I did very well. As I was driving home and climbing up an overpass, a new song came on the radio. The song was "Fool on the hill!" I must admit it caught my attention and made me wonder about my negotiating skills.

Flight Log: April 5, 1968 "Junction Run"
Aircraft Commander – John Sellmer
Navigator – Bernard Martin

I enjoyed the Junction Runs, because, like the Embassy Run, we got to keep the same airplane all the way around. That meant our layovers could be scheduled down to the hour of departure.

I really enjoyed flying with John Sellmer. John was just three or four years older than me, but for some reason he assumed a "Big Brother" role with me. He was always look- ing out for me.

It was a rare treat to be able to fly into Tehran. I don't know too many people who have been there. Of course the Shah was still alive and in power back then, and he was friendly to the US.

One of my 67C Classmates, Ahmad Separi, was from Iran. He was flying F-5's out of some base around there, but I didn't know which one. We were only there a couple of hours, so I didn't get a chance to look him up. I can't help but wonder if he is still alive. After the Shah was deposed, they rounded up all those loyal to him and shot or imprisoned them.

When we took off out of Tehran John was feeling his oats. He pulled the nose up for a steep climb out and the next thing we knew we were getting the stick shaker, indicating an impending stall. I looked over at him and said, "John, I think you might better lower the nose just a tad bit!" He laughed, but he did it.

We laid over in Madrid on the way out on this trip, and we went to La Casa Botine for some roast suckling pig. It was as delicious as it was the first time. We also laid over in Frankfurt twice. We found one of those famous giant beer garden places and spent a great evening there. We watched a lederhosen band and were amazed at the beer drinking capacity of those Germans. I certainly would not want to try to keep up with them.

Sheila was starting to look like she could have that baby any day now. I was so reluctant to go out again, but I knew there would be another trip in my immediate future.

Sheila and I had told Mike Pettit, who worked in Crew Scheduling, that she was due to have the baby early in May. Mike arranged for me to get my Annual Simulator Recurrent Training during that time. That would keep me home for at least a few days.

Sheila and I decided to go out for dinner at the officer's club the first night I was home. As we were leaving the base we saw a small white dog on the side of the road. It was all muddy and wet and scared and shaking. I stopped the car, got a towel out of the trunk, and wrapped the puppy in it. I gave her to Sheila to hold and she cradled that sweet little dog like it was the baby she was expecting. I knew Sheila loved cats because she had one when we were married. His name was Diablo. Unfortunately, I was violently allergic to cats back then and Diablo had to stay with her parents. That day I got a glimpse of how much Sheila truly loves all little animals. She immediately gave this one a name. It was Precious Puppy or PP for short!

We discovered that this dog was a Maltese and a very expensive one at that. We learned this through the vet who checked her out for us. We didn't want to bring a diseased dog into the house with a newborn baby. We had to leave word with the vet at the base that we had found the dog, since it obviously belonged to someone. Sure enough, three days later someone came around for the dog. When she saw the person, PP tried to run away. We were reluctant to give her back because we both had a very bad feeling about how that person treated their dog. But there was nothing we could do. Sheila cried for two days over that puppy.

Flight Log: April 29 – May 3
Instructor Pilot – Major Scott
Annual Simulator Recurrent Training

On my second day in the Simulator I started having some severe pain in my scrotum. I was concerned it might be cancer. It hurt that badly. I went straight to the flight surgeon after I finished my simulator check ride. He said I had a bad urinary tract infection. He gave me some strong antibiotics and grounded me for a minimum of two weeks. That could not have come at a better time.

On the evening of May 3 Sheila was feeling restless, and she said she would like to take a walk. There was a dirt road that ran along and behind the apartments. It circled the swamp and was a beautiful walk. There were huge cypress and oak trees all over the place. It was one of the most beautiful and memorable walks. We didn't know it at the time, but the next day our lives were going to change wonderfully. We would be the parents of a bouncing baby girl!

Chapter 11

Our Daughter Theresa Lynn is Born!

Sheila and I both moped around the apartment all day on May 4. I was not feeling well because I had that infection, and she was not feeling well because she was about to have her first child!

Around six in the evening she said, "Mike, my water just broke and I am starting to have contractions. I think it's time to go to the hospital." I was ready to go in three minutes!

All military families in Charleston used the Navy Hospital for childbirth and other more serious things. It was the best hospital in Charleston. I called the Navy base and said we were on the way. We got there around 6:30. They checked Sheila out and said it would be a little while before she was ready for the delivery room. I stayed with her and held her hand as the contractions continued. I felt guilty for causing her this pain.

Around 10:30 the doctor decided it was time for the baby to be born. They took Sheila into the delivery room and pointed me to the reception area. I can use one word to describe the reception area and that word is bleak! There was nothing in there but hard straight back metal chairs. There weren't even any windows. But there was a phone hanging on the wall. I used it to call my neighbor Mary. I asked her to come sit with me and she did. I did some pretty heavy praying during that wait.

Theresa was born after 11:00 that night. The doctor came in and announced that I had a healthy baby daughter and that mother and child were doing fine. I asked the doctor when I could see them and he said, "The nurse will come get you in a few minutes. We are cleaning the baby up so she will be pretty for her Daddy."

They took me to the nursery first, so I could see Theresa. She was lying on her right side, facing me. When I first looked at her both her eyes were wide open. But, I swear to this day, the next thing I saw was her winking at me! It was love at first sight.

Sheila was still on the gurney when I got to her. She looked like she had been through hell but she was smiling. I leaned over, kissed her, and said, "Thank you for the beautiful baby. I love you Sheila." I said a silent prayer of thanksgiving for both of them.

It was after midnight in Charleston, but it was still 11:00 in West Orange and Dallas. When we got to the hospital I made calls to Mom and Dad and to Stan and Winnie Niedzwiecki. I told them they were about to become grandparents and that I would call back when the baby was born. They all said to call no matter how late it was. So I did. Everyone was delighted with the news. Mother said she would catch the first flight to Atlanta the next day. She was going to be there to help Sheila with the baby for the first couple of weeks.

I went home and slept like a dead man. I was at the hospital bright and early the next day with a dozen roses. I got to hold Theresa that time. I stayed there a while and then I told Sheila I was going to the airport to pick up Mother. On the third day we took Sheila and Theresa home from the hospital.

Home with our baby girl

First portrait of our baby girl

Flight Log: May 17, 1968

Flight Examiner – Major Bill Hollman
Annual Proficiency Check ride

I went back to the Flight Surgeon and he put me back on flight status. My proficiency check ride went well too. So far I was not having any problems in the C-141 program.

I had eight days off after this check ride. This time off was ideal for getting accommodated to having an infant in the house. The crying at anytime twenty-four hours a day was hard to get used to. Mom was there with us and she was such a great help to Sheila. I just kind of wandered around the apartment looking bewildered.

Flight Log: May 26, 1968
AC – Captain William E Jones
Nav – Dick Avery

On our inbound layover at Elmendorf while down in the Stag Bar, I looked over at the bar, and there stood Louis "Louie" Nye. Louie was very popular on the Steve Allen show in those days. I approached him, saying, "Excuse me Sir, but aren't you Gordon Hathaway from Manhattan?"

He laughed and said, in his famous Gordon Hathaway accent, "Thanks a lot Lieutenant!"

We shook hands and had a nice visit. I got to tell him how much my friend Don Walker and I enjoyed his show when we were in high school. In fact, Don and I used to recreate the skits we saw the next day at school.

It was sometime during this time off that I reluctantly took Mom back to the airport for her flight home. She had been such a great help to Sheila, and the meals she cooked were delicious. Mother and Theresa bonded for life on this first meeting, and that bond would remain very strong throughout the rest of my Mother's life.

Flight Log: June 14, 1968 "East Coast Shuttle"
Aircraft Commander – General William V McBride

General McBride was our Wing Commander and the highest-ranking person I flew with in my Air Force career. This was the second time I got to fly with a Wing Commander, the first time being Colonel Chester J. Butcher in the T-38 at Webb.

I learned that, when the General called and scheduled himself for this trip, they tried to schedule an Instructor Pilot with him. He would have nothing to do with that. He told them, "I want a copilot to fly with me. I want to see how well you are training your copilots." Scheduling chose me to go with him.

The General was a very good pilot and a personable man. We got along great on this trip. He asked me how close I was to making aircraft commander and I said, "Sir, I have over fifteen hundred hours now and I am closing in on the two thousand that are required. I should be able to check out in November or December.

"Well Mike, you will be ready by then!"

"General, I am ready now!"

He laughed.

At the end of the trip he said, "Mike, we are having a Parade in Review next week. I have decided I want you to be the Adjutant for that parade."

The adjutant plays a major role in a Parade in Review, and he is quite visible in the proceedings. He calls out "Sound adjutant's call! And then "Report." After all squadrons report in he says, "All squadrons present or accounted for sir!" Then he does a quick time and a half march to another position on the parade grounds. It is a very conspicuous walk and is kind of funny to watch. I think the General just wanted to watch my big ass do that walk.

I said, "But Sir, I am just a lowly ROTC Graduate. We have several Air Force Academy graduates in the 76th who would be much better at that than me."

He looked over at me, raised an eyebrow for emphasis and said, "Nope, I've made my choice and you are it. Come by my office tomorrow and my secretary will have a manual on parade protocol waiting for you."

And that was that. You don't say no to a General. By the way, this particular General went on to become the Deputy Chief of Staff of the United States Air Force.

The parade went off without a hitch and after it was over he said, "Nice job Lieutenant Trahan. From now on, as long as you are here, you are my permanent adjutant! "And then he laughed!

It was about this time that Sheila and I had a long talk about our future. I thought, at the time, that I would be in Charleston at least another two and half years to complete my four-year tour. That meant two and a half more years of this kind of hectic schedule. The excessive time away and short times between trips was getting the best of us.

Sheila and I talked about putting in paperwork to get out of the Air Force when my five-year commitment was up. I told her that my chances of getting into fighters had gone by the wayside when I chose transports, and if I was going to fly this kind of airplane in this kind of mission from now on, I might as well do it for the airlines. At least in the civilian world I would have more control over my schedule and I definitely would get paid a lot more. Sheila had flown for Braniff Airlines so she knew the potential there. She agreed that we should get out of the Air Force. The next morning I went to the base Personnel office and put in my separation paper work. Ironically, it was also about this time that I was promoted to Captain. I really liked that rank!

Flight Log: July 5, 1968
Aircraft Commander – Major Bob Waring
Navigator – Robert George

One of the great benefits of going through Anchorage, Alaska was the opportunity to bring home some pretty nice wild meat and seafood. We could get packages of fresh or smoked salmon, moose meat, elk, and especially King Crab. We could buy a ten-pound box of frozen king crab legs for about a dollar a pound. There must have been a great sale on king crab this trip because everyone on the crew bought at least two or three boxes.

The crab was frozen when we got it, and to keep it frozen we stored it in the compartments that covered the landing gear. I think we had twenty or thirty boxes of crab in there on this trip. The gear cover was not insulated or pressurized, so the minus 55 degree temperatures at altitude permeated the compartments where the crab was and kept it frozen.

We thought we were going to make a quick stop at Dover on the way home, but after landing something broke in the airplane. They didn't have a replacement part there so we were told to go into crew rest and they would call us when the airplane was ready to go.

We had been sleeping about four hours when we got a call from the Chief of Maintenance. He said, "Guys, you better come out to your airplane. It is stinking up the entire ramp out here." We had forgotten about the king crab legs and they had thawed out and were really starting to smell. That all went into the trashcan.

When I got back from that trip I had two weeks of office duty. My boss, Major Dick Glogowski, spent the first week teaching me how to interpret and write reports on the training statistics we kept on all crewmembers. It was an important job because we were the last line of defense when it came to ensuring that all our people were current on their requirements.

Flight Log: July 30, 1968 "East Coast Shuttle"
Aircraft Commander – Major Joe Sicliano

It was on this trip where I first heard the words Operation Palace Cobra, a program where the Air Force was identifying first assignment pilots, like me, for reassignment to Vietnam. Apparently a big buildup in forces was coming up and PACAF needed experienced pilots to fill some jobs. Once your name was on the Palace Cobra list, it was just a matter of time before you got orders to Vietnam. When we got back to the squadron that afternoon I checked, and sure enough, my name was on it.

Flight Log: August 9, 1968
Aircraft Commander – John Sellmer

Trip #41 was one of the oddest trips of my entire MAC Career. John Sellmer and I decided to take our golf clubs on this trip, so we could play golf at some of the European bases. We got to Madrid and played the Torrejon AFB course. When we got in we learned that our trip the rest of the way through Europe had been cancelled and we were to fly back home to Charleston the next day. All we did on that trip was fly to Spain, play golf, and fly home.

Chapter 12

Aircraft Commander – At Long Last

Flight Log: August 16,1968
Local Flight – Aircraft Commander Training
Instructor Pilot – Captain Bill Thalberg

My total Air Force time was approaching two thousand hours, so I had finally been put in the Aircraft Commander pipeline. I had waited two years for this. This was my first AC Training Ride to prepare me for my AC Maneuvers Check Ride. Bill gave me a good workout.

Flight Log: August 17, 1968
Aircraft Commander – Capt Dick Gabrielson

The highlight of this trip was the first leg. I was able to call my Biloxi friends, Rodney and Georgette Mattina, and tell them I would be landing in Gulfport, Mississippi in a C-141. I invited them to come out for a visit while we loaded our cargo. I was able to give them a tour of the airplane, which was pretty special. We all remembered the time I flew into there in my little Cessna 140 to fly Rodney to Orange.

Flight Log: August 31, 1968
Aircraft Commander – Major Burke

This was an historic trip. We were called out because of riots at the Democratic National Convention in Chicago where some anti-war radicals were trying to disrupt the proceedings. We flew to Forbes AFB and picked up a load of National Guard troops and took them to O'Hare. Then we went to Peterson AFB and got another load and took them to O'Hare. We wound up in Austin at Bergstrom AFB that night, and flew home the next day. This was another one of those "Forest Gump" type brushes with history.

Flight Log: September 3, 1968
Aircraft Commander – Major Jack Schmidt
Navigator – Chuck Fenton

When Jack found out I was getting checked out as an Aircraft Commander he gave me as many pointers as he could on this trip. I was no longer his copilot. I was a guy on his way up the ladder, and I appreciated that from Jack. We had a lot of discussions about decision-making and I learned a lot on this trip.

Flight Log: October 7, 1968
Local Flight – AC Training Flight #2
Instructor Pilot – Bert Pekarek

Everything was going smoothly on my second AC

Training Flight until we started having oil pressure problems in one of the engines. We decided to cut the mission
short and land so the mechanics could check the engine out.
It was a good thing we did. The oil pump was starting to fail.

Flight Log: October 25, 1968
Aircraft Commander – L/Col Ramsey
Navigator – Neil Murton

This was NOT the typical PACAF trip. When we landed
at Saigon we were told to run the before start checklist and
be ready to hit the start button the instant our "passenger"
got to the airplane. They would not tell us who he was!

When he entered the cockpit, all we could see were
stars on his shoulder boards. It was Four Star General
Creighton Abrams, the Supreme Commander of the Pacific
Forces. He was on his way to Washington for a secret meeting with the President. He spent some time on the jump seat
visiting with us. In spite of his lofty rank, he was a very con-
genial man. We left him and the airplane in Okinawa, where
they continued on with the flight. We went into crew rest.

On our flight from Kadena to Elmendorf we received an
emergency call from Shemya Island. Shemya is a remote out-
post and is very close to the Russian border. We always
stayed well south of that place on our fights across the North
Pacific, but not this night.

The caller said they had a man on the island that had a
hot appendix and needed surgery at Elmendorf. We had to
call our Command Post and authenticate this flight plan
change using the secret codes we carried around all the time.
Everything checked out and we descended for an approach.

The weather was solid overcast, and it was the middle of the night. When we broke out of the clouds at 300 feet all we could see were the runway lights. That was the blackest night I have ever flown in. We were over the water and it felt like we were coming in to land on a carrier. Colonel Ramsey made the approach and landing and he had to fight a pretty strong crosswind to get us down. We loaded up the passenger, refueled the airplane and departed for Elmendorf. The man was alive when we landed. I never found out if he stayed that way.

Flight Log: November 5, 1968
Instructor Pilot – Major Jack Schmidt

MAC Trip 47 turned out to be a 409 Aircraft Commander Training Flight for me. We kept the airplane throughout the trip and we hit a lot of different bases to give me experience at some new places.

This was my first and only South Pacific trip westbound. I had flown the South Pacific eastbound when I flew the Embassy run. It was a lot different than flying the bleak, cold, desolate North Pacific.

When we got to Hawaii we hit a few of the islands. We did some touch-and-go landings on the big island of Hawaii.

Jack just continued the training he started giving me a couple of trips ago. I was happy to have him as my IP for this final phase of my line training.

Flight Log: November 19, 1968
Local Flight – Local – AC Training Flight #3

Instructor Pilot - Don Smock

This flight was a tune up for my Annual Instrument Check AND my Aircraft Commander Check Ride. Everything went well, and Don recommended me for the check ride.

When we got back to the squadron I was notified that my separation from the Air Force had been approved. It was so ironic that this notification came on the same day I was finishing my training for Aircraft Commander in the C-141. My DOS (Date of Separation) was 22 October 1970. That was exactly five years to the day after I entered the Air Force.

I got an invitation to General McBride's office after I put my DOS paperwork in. I was a Regular Officer by virtue of my being an Honor Graduate in ROTC. I had been offered and had accepted a regular commission as opposed to a Reserve Officer Commission when I was in Pilot Training. Apparently I had some kind of future in the Air Force.

General McBride said, "I want you to tell me why you are throwing away this opportunity Mike. I don't want to hear a bunch of negatives either. I want to hear positive reasons why you are leaving the Air Force."

"Sir, I made a colossal mistake when I graduated from Undergraduate Pilot Training. I was ranked right at the top of my class and I could have had any assignment in the list. I passed up a fighter assignment for C-141's. There were several valid reasons for doing that, but it was a mistake. I should have flown fighters. And now there doesn't seem to be any way for me to get into them. It appears I am stuck in transports for the rest of my career. If I thought I could eventually fly Air Force One that would be fine. But I don't think that will ever happen."

I paused a minute to formulate my words. "Now, having said that, I must say that it has been very interesting flying in MAC. I have learned things here that I could never have learned anywhere else, and I appreciate that. I won't deny that I am going to try to get into the airlines when my tour is up. I am sure any airline would be happy to have someone with nearly two thousand hours of C-141 time. My wife Sheila and I have discussed this thoroughly, and we just feel we would be happier in the civilian world. All this time away has been very hard on both of us. She worked for Braniff before we got married and she knows that business. I hope I have answered your question satisfactorily Sir."

He leaned back in his chair, smiled and said, "Here Mike, have a cigar. Yes, I can see your reasons for leaving and they are valid. You learned one good lesson in the Air Force. You better be damn sure of your choice when you are given one, because you will have to live with that choice the rest of your career. I will approve your DOS (Date of Separation) request, with regrets, and I wish you the best in your future career. Thanks for coming in."

He got up from his chair and we shook hands. I stepped back, saluted, and exited his office. I felt good that the General would take forty-five minutes out of his day to ask me what I thought.

Flight Log: November 20, 1968
Local Flight – Local – AC Check Ride
Flight Examiner – Major Holman

I passed my Aircraft Commander Maneuvers Check Ride exactly two years after I entered training in the C-141.

The prize had always been to be the Aircraft Commander and have my own crew. I paid my dues. My logbook showed exactly 2011 hours of Air Force time and that was what the 437th Military Airlift Wing required if you wanted to be an AC. I had just spent two years and 1750 hours of On-The-Job-Training. I thought it was a pretty bad case of overkill.

Flight Log: November 23, 1968
Aircraft Commander Line Check
Flight Examiner – Major Don Smock
Lieutenant Colonel Hennis – AC Outbound
Capt Mike Trahan – AC Inbound

Mike in left seat on A/C Line Check

Colonel Hennis flew as Aircraft Commander on the outbound leg of the trip. After we landed at Danang I climbed into the left seat and took command. On my first takeoff as Aircraft Commander I had to shut down an engine. Right after V1 (The go-no-go speed) we got a starter valve open light. The danger here is an engine fire if the valve is actually open, and there was no way to know for sure. My first commands were "Gear up, Shut down Engine #4, and Engine Failure Checklist." I told the Flight Examiner that I elected to go Okinawa instead of returning to Danang. I said, "We still have three good engines, we don't have any cargo, and they have maintenance at Kadena." He concurred with my decision. It was a judgment call.

The mechanics in Kadena replaced the starter valve indicator light and the airplane was ready to go when we were.

We flew to Yokota on the next leg. While we were in Crew Rest they configured our airplane for a Medical Evacuation Flight. We had been flying the same airplane on this trip, but we were going to lose it when we got to Alaska. It was going to continue on with another crew so they could get the injured soldiers home.

Just before we boarded the wounded, my Flight Engineer came to me and said we had a problem with the brake on one of the main wheels. I had the command post delay boarding, because it was cold as hell and I didn't want those guys out there freezing and uncomfortable while they worked on the airplane. I took a two-hour delay to get it fixed. In less than thirty minutes this Lieutenant Colonel was breathing down my neck. He was demanding to know exactly when we were going to board. I calmly said, "Sir, we will board when I am certain this airplane is ready to go, and not until then." He was frustrated but there was nothing he could do.

The rest of the trip went very well and when we landed at Elmendorf Major Smock said, "Congratulations Mike! You are now the newest Aircraft Commander in the Military Airlift Command!" We had a celebratory dinner in the maim dining room of the Elmendorf Officer's Club that night. I called Sheila from the BOQ to tell her the good news.

Now that I was Aircraft Commander Qualified at long last, I was so looking forward to enjoying some trips in command.

**Top: Henning, Trahan, Smock, Bailey
Bottom: Loadmasters and Flight Engineers**

When I got home from the trip Sheila and I celebrated with a night out on the town. We called Jerry and Dee Keyser and asked them to join us. We went to a Mexican Restaurant in downtown Charleston.

One week later Colonel Hennis and I met the Wing Certification Board to be certified as Aircraft Commanders. I think it was more of a congratulatory ceremony than anything. General McBride presided, and members of his Wing Staff, including our Squadron Commander, were on the board.

The General asked me if I had any comments about the AC Upgrade Program. I said, "Yes sir, I do! As you know, our Wing requires two thousand hours of Air Force time before we can upgrade to AC. All the other MAC Wings require only fifteen hundred hours. Because of that, I had to wait six extra months for my chance to check out, in comparison to my peers at the other wings. That is my only criticism Sir. Other than that, once I got into the upgrade program, I thought it was thorough and that it prepared me well for the job I was striving for. Thank you!"

General McBride surprised me with his next statement. He said, "Captain Trahan, I understand your frustrations. I have flown with you, and I have tracked your progress, and I am very confident you could have handled the Aircraft Commander job at fifteen hundred hours. However, this wing is blessed with an abundance of experienced AC's and ours is the best safety record in the Military Airlift Command. So, it is my judgment that we give our copilots more experience before turning them loose with their own crew." I said, "I understand Sir. Thank you." With that he signaled the board was over, and all the members came out and shook hands with Col Hennis and me.

On the way out I walked by the desk of the general's secretary. She signaled for me to stop and said, "Captain Trahan, I have an urgent message for you to call personnel!" I borrowed her phone and called them right away. The voice on the other end of the line said, "Captain Trahan, you have orders. You are being assigned to the 4th Special Operations Squadron in Nha Trang, Vietnam. You will be flying the AC-47 Gunship. You are to report to Global Survival School on 3

February 1969!"

I turned around and walked right back into the boardroom, where the General and all the other Colonels were still milling around. I walked up to General McBride and said, "Well General, I just learned that I have flown my LAST MAC flight. I've been notified that I have orders to Vietnam. I will barely have enough time to relocate my family in Texas before I have to go to Survival School!"

He got a shocked look on his face and said, "Mike, I'm sorry you are not going to get to enjoy the benefits of all your work here. Thank you for your fine contributions to this Wing and to the 76th Squadron. Good luck Son!" And that was the end of my tour in the Airlift Command.

Last mission in the C-141

Sheila was so excited when I got home that evening.

She had cooked a special meal to celebrate my upgrade to Aircraft Commander. I hated to have to tell her I would not get to fly another trip as a C-141 Aircraft Commander, because I had orders to go to Vietnam. She was taken aback by this devastating news, but she soon composed herself. We knew it was only a matter of time, after my name went on the Palace Cobra list, that I would get a Vietnam assignment. We just didn't expect it to happen so soon.

"Oh Mike, I am so sorry. I know how hard you have worked for this. What a shame you are not going to get to fly at least a few trips as AC."

"Well Honey, that's the story of my life isn't it? I work like hell to achieve a goal, and once I get there, or almost there, it gets jerked away from me. I endured two years and nearly two thousand hours of on the job training for just ONE lousy trip, and that trip was my check ride!

I felt myself starting to become a little bitter about this and I was so tempted to just yell at the top of my lungs, "Lord, why do you keep screwing with my life like this?" But every time I got that impulse I would look back at all the disappointments I've had and what those disappointments eventually led to. When it happened this time I just let it go - again.

I didn't like it much, but I did believe that this was all part of God's grand plan for me, and that the timing of it was critical. That became clear to me a year and a half later.

My mind was reeling when I went to bed that night. So much had changed in the blink of an eye. I woke that morning thrilled that I was getting certified as an Aircraft Commander and went to bed knowing that I was on my way to war.

Strangely, my emotions went from disappointment, to excitement, to dread and back and forth. I was actually glad that, after two years of flying into Vietnam, unarmed and unable to shoot back at those bastards who had been taking potshots at me, I now would be flying an airplane that could kick their asses! I was looking forward to that,

I dreaded the separation from Sheila and Theresa. My baby girl was almost a year old, and I would not get to be there for her birthday. My overseas date was April and her birthday was in May. I felt terrible that Sheila was going to have to spend all that time alone. I figured up my time away since we were married, and when I threw in another twelve months for Vietnam, I realized I would have been gone twenty-seven of our first thirty-six months of marriage.

Chapter 13

Preparing To Go To War

First family portrait
Photo by T.L. Gunn

Sheila and I had a lot to take care of. We had to find a place for her and the baby to stay while I was in Vietnam. We also had to figure out where they would stay while I was at AC-47 training. That school was in Alexandria, Louisiana and it was an unaccompanied tour. I was hoping we could find some way for them to be in Alexandria with me.

After I got my orders the squadron put me on ground duty. They let me work in the Training Department the entire month of December. I had a lot of out-processing to do and a lot of loose ends to tie up. This allowed me time to take care of arrangements for my family.

My travel orders were very generous. I was given specific dates where I had to be someplace, but other than that I was on my own, and I was not being charged any leave time for it.

After Christmas, the Air Force movers packed up all our household goods and transported them to storage. We decided to get a place for Sheila and Theresa to stay in San Angelo while I was gone, so our household goods would be waiting for us there. Her parents and some aunts and uncles lived in San Angelo, and it was a logical place for her to be.

I checked out of the Squadron the day after Christmas and we were on our way home. We were not the only ones with orders. Mike Pettit, Craig Morrison, Jerry Keyser and Travis Scott also had orders. Mike got an assignment on the C-7 Caribou. Craig got a Forward Air Controller assignment. He would be flying the O-2 Birddog. Jerry and Travis got an assignment with Air Rescue. They would be flying Jolly Green Giant helicopters. Ray Caracciolo was also up for an assignment, but he had a health problem and didn't go.

We drove out to San Angelo first. We had to secure a house for them to live in. There was a realtor in the family, and she had been working on it even before we got there. She showed us a couple of places, but we liked the one on Oxford Street best.

We signed the lease, paid the deposit, and moved our furniture in. We had to do all this now, because I would not have much time after I finished AC-47 School. We visited with her parents and the other members of the Corbell family. I told them we would come back there and stay a while after I finished AC-47 training and before I left for Vietnam.

After New Year's we drove to West Orange. I had told my parents earlier that I would be training at England AFB in Alexandria, Louisiana. I also told them that since this was an unaccompanied tour, the Air Force would not provide housing, nor would they pay a housing allowance for Sheila and Theresa to stay with me.

"I hope we can find an apartment or something. I just can't imagine spending my last few months home without them."

Dad said, "Don't worry one minute about that Mike. They will be with you during your training."

When we got to West Orange one of the first things Dad said was, "We've found a place for you to stay in Alexandria!" He had been talking with our friend Harry Sutton, and he told Harry we were looking for a place to stay for a couple of months while I trained in Alexandria. Harry had some business interests in Alexandria and he knew a lot of people there. One of his Alexandria friends was Victor Moreau. Vic was a corporate pilot who lived on a ranch not far from England Air Force Base. Harry asked Vic if he knew of a place where we could stay.

Vic replied, "I have a garage apartment behind my house. My mother-in-law used to stay there. It hasn't been used in a while and it needs a thorough cleaning, but they can stay there if they want to."

Harry took a look at the place the next time he was up there and told Dad it would be fine for us. He told Victor we wanted it.

A few days after we got to West Orange we asked Mom to babysit Theresa so we could run up to Alexandria and look at the apartment. We brought some brooms, mops, and cleaning supplies with us.

When we got to the address we were overwhelmed at what we saw. Victor and Betty Moreau lived on one of the most beautiful ranches in that part of the country. They had a grand main house and the garage apartment was set apart, about fifty yards behind the house. They greeted us with open arms and then they took us out and showed us the apartment.

We liked it right away. It was actually a two-car garage. The doors had been removed and Vic built a wall with a couple of windows and a door. In the right hand corner on the backside was a little kitchen area. It was small but good enough to cook our meals on. There was a double bed for us, and Betty had heard that we had an infant with us. She lent us the bed she had used for her babies. There was a small closet area and one corner was closed off for the bathroom. It had a small shower, a sink and a commode, but again, it was enough for our needs. Other than needing a little mopping and dusting, the place was actually in good shape.

I told Vic we would love to stay there and I asked him how much it would cost.

"Aw, I don't know Mike. Why don't you just fill up the propane tank and pay the electric bill when you leave and we'll call it even?" I said that would be just fine. I told him I had to go to Global Survival Training in February, but that we would be back for AC-47 training in early March.

"That will be fine Mike. The apartment is not going anyplace. We are looking forward to having you here with us for a while."

Sheila and I drove back to Orange, where we waited until it was time for me to go to Global Survival School. I did a little flying with Ed Feuge in his Cessna 182 while we were sitting around. I had not flown light airplanes in quite a while. We went up and flew a few approaches. It was good to fly with Ed again after three years in the Air Force.

Irony of ironies, when I arrived at Fairchild forty-eight inches of snow was piled on the ground. I thought I was going to survival school for Southeast Asia, where it doesn't ever snow. When I got there I learned that this was just Phase One of my survival training. I would get Jungle Survival Training in the Philippines on the way to Vietnam.

This school was mostly about escaping, evading, and if necessary, surviving capture. The most intense part of the program was a mock POW Compound that they put us in. Trust me, we got a very good taste of what it might be like to be a POW in North Vietnam. We were taught how to resist interrogation to the extent possible. We learned a lot about the Uniform Code of Military Justice and what was expected of us if we were captured. Under the Geneva Convention we were only required to give our Name, Rank, and Serial Number and we were encouraged to give only that.

Part of the school was a two day survival trek, but for some reason I didn't have to go on that, and I was just as happy about it. The school only lasted a week, and I was back home by February 10. We didn't have to be in Alexandria for AC-47 ground school until February 25, so we enjoyed another two weeks off.

Of all the bases in the United States that were training pilots for Vietnam assignments, England AFB was the closest one to West Orange, Texas. That could not have been more convenient for us and I don't think it was just a coincidence. I think it was one of those "God things!"

It didn't take us long to settle into life at Moreau's farm. The little garage apartment was perfect for the three of us. I was so happy that I could have Sheila and Theresa there with me. One day we were outside, I saw this view of Sheila and Theresa and I just snapped a picture, without saying anything to them. The picture I got is my all-time favorite shot of the two of them, and it sat on my night table my entire year in Vietnam.

Theresa and Sheila at Moreau's Ranch

As I mentioned before, the AC-47 was my first choice out of all the assignments I could have had, so I was glad to get it. If I could not have a fighter, I at least wanted an airplane that could shoot back! I thought it was interesting that I had gone from the newest and most modern transport aircraft in the Air Force, to the oldest one in the fleet. The Douglas C-47 Dakota had been in the inventory since World War II. That airplane did some amazing work in Europe and elsewhere. It was used for parachute drops, towing gliders, transporting personnel, and finally hauling cargo in the China, Burma, and India corridor. This mission was also known as flying "The Hump" because of the huge mountains these airplanes had to fly over in that mission.

If this airplane looks familiar is should, because it is identical to the airplane I flew in for Mr. Edgar Brown. The Air Force, the Airlines, and even some individuals flew this airplane well into the seventies. Some of them are still flying today. In the civilian world the Dakota is known as the DC-3. The Air Force designates it the C-47. They are the same airplane with different names. Pilots who flew it just called it "The Three." The DC-3 is a legend in aviation lore. I am glad I got to fly this classic airplane.

England Air Force Base was pretty laid back for an Air Force Base. The pace of life there was fairly slow and unhurried, unlike a lot of bases I had visited. I think it was probably the Louisiana influence!

In addition to the C-47 and AC-47 Schools, there was also an F-100 Fighter Squadron based there. I got a chance to visit with some of the F-100 pilots. Some had just come home from Vietnam and some were just getting ready to leave. At that time they were pretty fired up about the mission they were flying over there and they had nothing but respect for the job I was going to be doing over there too. One returning veteran said, "Mike, I've seen Spooky work, close up, and that thing is awesome! They do a great job providing night close air support for the troops over there!"

Night? Did he say night? Until that moment I didn't realize that ALL my missions in the AC-47 would be flown at night. There was a good reason for this. They sent some Spooky gunships out on a daytime mission and before they could call them off the target, three of them were shot down.

The AC-47 uses side firing gunnery. The guns are mounted in the cabin and shoot out the left side of the aircraft. That means the airplane flies around the target in a relatively constant circle. Well, it doesn't take a genius gunner to figure out that firing solution. After that, all the Spooky missions were flown at night, and they proved to be quite effective.

Ground school went relatively smoothly. An airplane, with systems that were designed in the late nineteen thirties, was not that complex. We were finished with ground school in two weeks. Then it was time to start transition training. I and another student drew Jim Yarwood for my instructor. He had been with the school a couple of years. Our first flight was March 13.

I was very pleased to learn that I was receiving training as an Aircraft Commander in this program. I guess upgrading in the C-141 on my last MAC flight was worth something. At least I would not have to wait to be in command on this airplane. Or so I thought!

Flight Log: March 10 – March 20, 1969
C-47 Transition Training
Total Flights: 8   Total Time: 20 hours

The first five flights consisted of mostly traffic pattern work. We shot a lot of touch and go landings during those first few hours. Yarwood was completely surprised when I mastered flying a tail wheel airplane right away.

"Hell, it usually takes me three rides to get my students where they can taxi the airplane."

It is fair to say that most Air Force pilots had never flown a tail wheel airplane. I told Jim I started out in tail draggers and that I had a little bit of time in the DC-3 before I got into the Air Force. He put me on the "accelerated syllabus" when he learned that.

I enjoyed the flights with Yarwood. They usually lasted two and a half to three and a half hours. I passed my contact check ride and we moved on to instrument flying. Even though I had just recently had an instrument check in the C-141, I had to have another one in this airplane. I passed that one too, and then it was time to move on to Gunnery Training.

The AC-47 gun configuration

As you can see in the picture, the AC-47 differs from the standard C-47 aircraft. The rear door has been removed from the aircraft to facilitate the launching of our parachute flares for illumination. The glass was removed from the back three windows and the guns stuck out of them. All three windows were behind the wing, so it did not interfere with the firing.

The guns are fix mounted on pods that are bolted to the floor. They are bore sighted to a World War II reticle sight mounted in the Aircraft Commander's side window. The Aircraft Commander aimed the guns by banking the aircraft.

We carried three Mini-Guns on the AC-47. The Mini-gun fired a 7.62 mm shell. Every fifth round was a tracer. The gun used the multiple rotating barrel technology that was developed in the Gattling Guns of the Old West. They were capable of firing at 3000 or 6000 rounds per minute. We carried 21,000 rounds of ammunition and twenty-four phosphorous flares on each mission. The flares put out two million candlepower of light each.

Two gunners manned the guns. Their job was to keep them loaded and clear them when they jammed. One loadmaster was in charge of the flares. He lit them and threw them out the door on command.

Ammo cans on the floor

Flight Log: March 21 – 24, 1969
AC-47 Gunnery Training
Two Daylight Missions

For this training we flew over to Fort Polk in Leesville and used their gunnery range. The basic technique for side firing gunnery was to fly at an altitude of 3000 feet above the ground. This gave us a slant range to the target of 4500 feet. There was a World War II gun sight mounted in the side cockpit window next to the left seat. The sight picture looked like this – (.) except the dot was centered. By slightly adjusting bank for wind, the pilot could stay on target pretty much all the way around the circle. This gave us great coverage and saturation. It was very effective for close air support when our troops were in contact with the enemy.

Our first two missions were daytime flights. This allowed us to see and become confident that the bullets were going where the gun sight was pointed. This became important when we started firing at night, because the tracers burned out about halfway to the target, and the illusion was that we were firing way short of the target. We had to trust the gun sight and not our senses.

Two thousand rounds sound like a lot, but at the rate of just 3000 rounds per minute, each one-second squeeze of the trigger was fifty rounds. We only had forty squeezes and we were out of ammo, but that was enough to learn how to hit the target.

Flight Log: March 26, 1969
AC-47 Gunnery Training
Firing Mission over Gulf of Mexico

For this mission we flew down to a training area off the Louisiana Gulf Coast. We dropped a target in the water. It was a floating device about four feet by four feet and painted a bright orange. By shooting at it in the water, we could tell exactly where our bullets were going. If there were no splashes in the water, then all of them were going into the target. It was very effective training and it allowed me to fine-tune my aim quite well.

We had some flares in the airplane that night, and it was dark on the way back to Alexandria. Our route took us right over my mother's old hometown of Loreauville, Louisiana. Loreauville is nestled right up next to the Atchafalaya Swamp and the residents there, at least the ones I know, are very devout Catholics. They are also very superstitious. I told the crew we could really get the Rosaries going down there if we dropped one of those parachute flares into the swamp. Those Cajuns would think it was either a UFO or an Angel come down from Heaven to get them. Good sense got the better of me and I didn't do it.

Flight Log: March 27, 1969
AC-47 Gunnery Training
Night Mission

We flew over to Fort Polk again this night and I got practice firing at a target illuminated by flare light. We would fly over the target area and determine the wind direction. Then, when we were on the upwind side of the target, we would drop a parachute flare. As it drifted toward the ground, it also drifted over the target and gave off plenty of light to see what we were shooting at.

It took me a few minutes to get used to that very bright light drifting down, while flying in a circle, at thirty degrees of bank and in otherwise pitch darkness. In addition to all these factors, the flares put off a lot of dense smoke. That was problematic for us too.

Flight Log: April 1, 1969
AC-47 Gunnery Training
Night Mission – Aircraft Commander Check Ride

This was my Aircraft Commander Check Ride in the AC-47. The flight examiner was Major Bennett. Everything went well, and I passed. I had one more ride to fly at England and then my training there was complete.

Flight Log: April 4, 1969
AC-47 Gunnery Training
Night Mission – Working with a Navigator

The goal of this mission was to train me to work with a full crew on the AC-47. For this one I had a copilot, a navigator, a flight engineer, two gunners, and a loadmaster. We were given a series of target coordinates on Fort Polk's gun range, and we had to go to each one, identify it, and destroy it. It was nice having the navigator helping me identify the target. When you are sending that many bullets at the ground, you better know exactly where they are going and whom they will be hitting.

The night before we left Alexandria, Vic and Betty invited us to dinner in their home. After we ate, I asked Vic how much I owed him for the propane and electricity and water we used. He put his hand on my shoulder and said, "Just come home from this war alive Mike. That will be payment enough for me!" I told him he would the third person I would call when I got home, after Sheila and my parents – and he was!

Sheila, Theresa, and I drove to West Orange on April 5. We spent a few days visiting Mom and Dad. While we were there we celebrated Theresa's First Birthday with a little party. Her birthday was not until May 4 but I wanted to be a part of it.

While we were in Orange, I learned that Larry David had joined the Army and that he was going to be shipping out to Vietnam the same time I was. Larry's father, Jules, and my Dad, threw a barbeque party for out two families. It was a going away party for Larry and me. They said, "When you boys come home we are going to throw you the biggest barbeque in the history of Orange, Texas.

I went around and said goodbye to some people. Of course I saw my grandparents, aunts uncles and cousins and friends. I went by Dr. Howard William's office and I said, "Well Howard, when I get back home I will be a civilian. I will be coming back to you for my Flight Physicals again." Howard had given me every physical I had taken since I was fifteen, except during my Air Force years. I also went by to see my old friend Father Herman Vincent. I got his blessing once again, and his promise to pray for me every day while I was over there.

We then drove out to San Angelo to get settled into the rent house. Stan and Winnie were delighted to see us. The two weeks before it was time for me to leave were a blur. I don't remember much at all about what we did during that time. I just know we held each other very close, because we knew, when I left home that I might not come back alive. That was not something we dwelled on, but it was in the back of our minds.

Mom and Dad drove to San Angelo to be with us for my last few days at home. They wanted to see me off the day I left. The morning they left to go back home we said goodbye in the driveway. I kissed Dad goodbye, and I hugged Mother for a long time. I started to say something and she stopped me. She couldn't stand it.

"I will pray for you Son, every day. I love you!" I kissed her goodbye, told her I loved her too and then they drove away. I turned to Sheila and realized that we both had tears in our eyes.

My flight was later that evening, so we just spent the day holding on to each other. Every time I looked at Theresa I would tear up. I knew she would be two years old when I saw her again. I knew I was going to miss my beautiful young wife terribly also. All too soon, it was time to go.

April 19, 1969 - The day I left for Vietnam

I had orders to report to Los Angeles International Airport on April 20 for my flight to Southeast Asia. I decided to go a day early and spend the night at my cousin Gene Pleassala's house. I didn't want to risk missing my flight and getting into trouble.

I would be flying a Military Charter to Clark AFB in the Philippines. I would spend a week at Clark going to Jungle Survival School. After that I would fly directly to Vietnam and join my squadron.

Chapter 14

And It's Of to War I Go

On April 20, 1969, I caught a Continental Charter from Los Angeles International Airport and flew to Hawaii. We refueled and flew on to Clark AFB. I had a few days off before Jungle Survival School started. I spent that time hanging out at the officer's club visiting with people.

As I have mentioned before, Clark was a major hub for Southeast Asia, and I ran into some MAC crewmembers I knew. I also ran into Craig Morrison and Mike Pettit. They were there for Jungle Survival School too. We all were headed for Vietnam. On a side note: The common nickname for Jungle Survival School was "Snake School." Charming, huh?

We had three days of classroom training in jungle survival techniques and on the third day they loaded us up in trucks and drove us about ten miles into the wildest jungle I've ever seen. I forget what we had with us, but I believe it was just what we would have had if we had bailed out there. I know I had a survival knife, and probably a radio.

The first part of this exercise was how to survive on what the jungle had to offer. We learned how to extract drinking water and food out of palm trees, how to eat grubs and roots, etc.

The second part of the exercise was "escape and evasion." When it started getting dark they didn't take us in. They took us to another remote looking area and said, "Okay men, go find a place to hide!" They gave us three "blood chits" to carry. If we were caught we were to give the little native guy one chit. Then we would hide again and try to do better. The third time we were caught we were captured! I got caught twice, but not the third time. I found a little cave and hid in it. God knows what else was in there with me. I was so exhausted at that point it didn't matter. I slept until the sun came up.

I have spent a few nights in the woods so this was not anything out of the ordinary for me, but these woods were deeper and wilder than any I had ever been in. My fellow survivors from the cities up north didn't fare so well. They are comfortable in the dangerous alleyways in their cities, and with all the giant rats there, but they nearly freaked out having to live with the creatures in this place. Any one of them could eat any one of those big city alley rats.

After they gathered us all up the next morning, they trucked us back to the base. We almost lost one guy. He found a cave too and he was still asleep at ten o'clock that morning. They started shooting guns and yelling for him to turn on his radio and call in, and he finally did. The lost guy was my buddy Craig Morrison from the 76th Squadron. He was the only one of us who had not been caught all night. He had all three of his chits when he got to the truck.

We had the rest of the day to clean up and rest up. I was told that my flight to Saigon was scheduled for May 4 and that I was free to just relax around Clark until that day.

I spent some time going to the Base Exchange. A lot of guys, who were on their way to Vietnam, were buying little tape recorders. They said it was a great way to communicate with their families. Most of them were buying cassette recorders. I mistakenly bought the reel type and it was a little more difficult for Sheila and my parents to operate.

My tour in Vietnam was filled with ironies, but this was probably the most ironic thing of all, and it happened on my first day there. I started my year in Vietnam on May 4, 1969, which happened to be my daughter Theresa's first birthday!

My first memory of that day was walking out the front door of the terminal and seeing an old Vietnamese man standing on the curb, pissing into the street! He was not trying to hide anything from anybody. It was like this was the most natural thing in the world for him to do.

I went to Base Transportation to arrange a flight to my unit. I was assigned to the 4th Special Operations Squadron – D Flight based at Nha Trang. My flight was scheduled for 0800 the next morning.

I could not find a picture of my D Flight Patch, so I used one from B Flight. My patch said, "4th SOS D Flt" and it had the words Nha Trang, Vietnam written at the bottom of it.

Nha Trang was the Headquarters for the 4th Special Operations Squadron. We had flights at Tan Son Nhut, Pleiku, Phu Cat, Danang, and Nha Trang. Our Squadron Commander was Lieutenant Colonel Adam Swigler. My immediate supervisor was D Flight Commander, Lieutenant Colonel Rod Woods, and the Flight Operations Officer was Major Louis "Lou" Longhenry.

Our mission call sign was Spooky. I don't know exactly where that name came from, but it fit our mission. We always worked at night, like a ghost would, and I know we scared the hell out of a lot of people.

Spooky emblem on our aircraft

When I got to Nha Trang on May 5, I checked in with the D Flight First Sergeant and signed into the flight. The first thing I said to him was, "Hello Sergeant, when can I go on leave and how do I request an early release from the Air Force?"

He laughed, "Well Captain Trahan, I see you are joining us with a gung ho attitude!"

"Sergeant, first things first!"

After I finished checking in I went to see Colonel Woods

and Major Longhenry. They asked me about my background and I told them I had just come from MAC where I was an Aircraft Commander on the C-141. I said I had two thousand and fifty hours of Air Force flying time. Then I asked the most logical question I could think of.

"So, when do I get to meet my crew?"

Major Longhenry said, "Not so fast Mike. We have to check you out in-country before we can turn you loose with your own crew."

"How long is the checkout Major?"

"Two hundred hours!"

I couldn't believe I was going to be stuck in the right seat again, for a while at least. That sure seemed like an excessive amount of time for a theater checkout. I was so ticked off I could not see straight, but I didn't let them know.

"Well then, I am ready to get started on that two hundred hours!"

I figured, if I flew my butt off and volunteered for extra flights, I might have my time in two months. I don't remember exactly why it took so long, but I didn't even get to fly my first mission until May 15.

I vaguely recall some problem with housing at Nha Trang. My room in the BOQ was still occupied and I had to wait for it. I was temporarily housed in a tent, and boy was that uncomfortable. It was Africa hot in there, even at night, and I could not sleep a wink. Someone suggested that I go over to the squadron alert room and sleep there during the day and that is what I did. That room was air-conditioned and it was only used at night. Major Longhenry said he would not fly me until I had suitable rest facilities.

I also remember some major problems getting my mail

service straightened out. I didn't hear from Sheila or my parents at all for three weeks. That was hard on all of us.

After eight days in that stiflingly hot tent I finally moved into my air-conditioned room in the BOQ. That room was about ten by ten and it had one door, no window, a single bunk bed, a nightstand, a small desk and a chair. There was a lamp on the nightstand and one on the desk. There was an open closet with a shelf on top of it. It was enough for the few clothes I had with me. It was Spartan, but that place felt like a palace to me after living in that tent.

My BOQ was one of the larger buildings on base. My room was upstairs on the north side of the building, which ran east and west. The latrine was located in the mid-section of the building. There was a row of sinks on one wall. On the back of that same wall was a row of urinals, then a row of stalls with commodes in them. The showers were in another room we entered through a big cased opening. The place was functional enough.

The Officer's Club at Nha Trang was pretty nice. We got to see quite a few floorshows. Most of the entertainers were Vietnamese and Thais, but occasionally an Australian band would come through. That was always a treat, because the Aussie women were always tall, blonde and beautiful. They looked like amazons when compared to the little Vietnamese and Thai women.

Typical Floor Show at Nha Trang

The Asian entertainers could not speak English but they sang in English – sort of! They learned to parrot the English words to the songs, and sometimes they really came out funny. For example, in the song Proud Mary, the words "rolling on the river" came out "lolling on the liver!" And the wonderful Frank Sinatra song sounded like this, "Stwangers in the night, exchanging gwances, wuvvers at first sight. Stwangers in the night, two wonweee people we were stwangers in the night and before we said hello, widdle did we know, wuv was just a gwance away, a warm exciting dance away." You get the picture!

I was wrong when I estimated that it would take two months to fly the 200 hours I needed. It took nearly twice that time. My Flight Log shows that I didn't check out as Aircraft Commander until August 27! I had exactly 176 hours of Combat Time when I checked out. I guess they waived twenty-four hours for me. Regardless, it was still another excruciating four months for me as a damn understudy sitting in the right seat! This was not how I envisioned my Air Force career would be.

I am now going to take you along with me as I recall some of the combat missions I flew in the AC-47. I want you to get a feel for what it was really like doing that. All of these flights are memorialized in my Flight Log Books, and fortunately I still have them for reference, so dates and minute details are at my fingertips. So come with me, and let's fly some of the most exciting missions that war had to offer.

Flight Log: May 15, 1969
Spooky 41   Airborne Alert Mission or "Cap"
Instructor Pilot – Major Loessburg

I was told to report to the Flight Briefing room at 17:00 hours for an Intelligence Briefing. We were briefed on known enemy movements in our area of operation, what we might expect that night, and we were given the results of the previous night's missions. If the letters "KBA" were used they meant "Killed By Artillery." In this case, the "artillery" was the AC-47. On some nights the KBA number was staggering.

A lot of the flights we flew were just Airborne Alert missions and not a shot was fired. There was a Spooky airborne at all hours of the night, ready to respond to any call for help. Spooky 41 took off at dusk and landed at midnight. Spooky 42 took off at midnight and landed at dawn. If the weather was bad we would stand alert in the alert bunkroom. We slept in our flight suits and we didn't even take off our boots. If we were called out for a TIC "Troops in Contact" Mission, we were ready to hit the ground running. We could be airborne in fifteen minutes or less.

My first mission was uneventful. We just droned around

the area for three hours. The navigator was monitoring several combat frequencies as well as our DASC "Direct Air Support Center" frequency. We did not fire a single round unless we were cleared to do so by the DASC.

Major Loessburg showed me some areas where I could expect action later on. These were the hot spots near Nha Trang. We also covered Cam Ranh Bay in our air alerts.

I had three more Airborne Alert "Cap" rides and finally got my Copilot checkout completed. I flew a few more "Cap" missions and we still had not fired a single shot. I thought the war had ended.

On June 3, 1969 I got a trip to ferry an airplane to Phu Cat Air Base. I flew that one with Major Richardson. That was my first daylight flight since I got there! We flew up there to bring an airplane to the AC-47 Flight at Phu Cat. They were short one and we had an extra.

We spent the night there and flew our airplane back to Nha Trang the next morning. I ran into Mike Pettit, from my old MAC Squadron, that evening. We had a great visit. He was flying C-7 Caribous out of Phu Cat.

Flight Log: June 9, 1969
Spooky 42   H&I (Harassment and Interdiction) Mission
Aircraft Commander: Captain Stubitts
Total time: 1+55   21,000 Rounds Fired 20 Flares

This was one of those H&I (Harassment and Interdiction) Missions. We called them shooting monkeys and coconuts, but we were actually firing at a suspected enemy location. Even if they weren't there, our flares lighting up the night and our bullets landing all around them sure messed up their night. Anyway, it was the first time we fired a round since I had gotten there. It was very quiet in the beginning of my tour, but it heated up later on.

Captain Stubitts was about my age. He had been in Vietnam nine months when I flew with him. I flew with Stubitts on my next five missions.

Flight Log: June 13, 1969
Spooky 42 TIC (Troops In Contact) Alert Scramble
Aircraft Commander: Captain Stubitts
Total time: 0+45   0 Rounds   4 Flares

When the scramble alert went off I thought we were going to see some troops in contact action. This was what I was waiting for. Troops in Contact or (TIC) is when our guys or the South Vietnamese Army had engaged the enemy in a fire fight and were calling for close air support from us!

We were directed over Hon Tre Island, which is right near the base. There was some suspected enemy activity along the shoreline and the army guys wanted us to illuminate the area with flares. Consequently, they didn't see anything, and we were released to go back and land.

Flight Log: June 14, 1969
Spooky 42   TIC Mission at Dalat
Aircraft Commander: Captain Stubitts
Navigator: Captain Schnatter
Total time: 4+00   21,000 Rounds 40 Flares

We had just gotten airborne when we got the call that there was TIC action at Dalat. Dalat was some distance away, so we boogied over there as fast as we could. We made it in time.

The ground spotters had a great location on the enemy troops and they described the area they were in. We popped a parachute flare and the area directly under us was exactly as they described. Stubbits fired 21, 000 rounds that night and I have to give him props, because he did a good job. We were able to stop the attack but we had to hang around there quite a while to do it. And that reminds me of something.

There were several things about the AC-47 Mission that made it particularly dangerous and different from other close air support missions. The most glaring danger was our time of exposure to enemy fire. Fighters and other close air support aircraft were over the target and long gone in a matter of seconds when they made their firing or bombing passes. We, on the other hand, flew around the area in a circle, sometimes for hours on end, at one hundred twenty knots! We also flew at three thousand feet above ground level. That was high enough to take away the threat of small arms fire, but we were vulnerable to fifty caliber and thirty-seven millimeter fire. Of course we would have been sitting ducks for a SAM (Surface to air missile). Fortunately we didn't operate in areas where SAM's were reported. That would have been suicide.

We did have the cover of darkness to protect us and when we darkened our airplane and turned off our red rotating beacon we were invisible. Of course the guys on the ground could still hear our engines, and they would shoot at the sound. That is when we would put the two propellers out of synchronization and the oscillating noise that created made it impossible to locate us by sound. The flares also offered protection for us. It was hard to see us in the darkness above that very bright light and through all that smoke. But still, the AC-47 mission had the highest percentage of aircraft to fleet size loss in the war. Remember, we only had five flights of four aircraft each, so the loss of two airplanes represented ten percent of our fleet. I believe there had been seven Spooky aircraft shot down before I got there. We lost one during my year over there.

Mini-Gun Firing – Photo taken from aircraft door.

Flight Log: June 14, 1969
Spooky 42 Regeneration   Troops in Contact
Aircraft Commander: Captain Stubitts
Navigator: Captain Schnatter
Total time: 2+15   21,000 Rounds 40 Flares

We had just finished reloading fuel, flares and ammunition when we were scrambled again. Going up again on the same mission call sign was called Mission Regeneration. This time there was some action just north of Nha Trang, along a major highway. One of our truck convoys had been attacked. We spent a couple of hours suppressing that attack too. It was a busy night for us. The sun was just coming up when we landed.

At our intelligence briefing the next night we learned that Stubitts had killed twenty-five of the enemy and wounded dozens more on the Dalat mission, and a dozen more on our second sortie. Because of the nature of the threat and the good work he did, Stubitts was put in for a Distinguished Flying Cross for that mission. I was too, but I refused the recommendation because I was just riding along. I figured I would have my chance when I got in the left seat.

The copilot's job, during these firing missions, was to keep the Aircraft Commander out of trouble. Specifically, he was there to keep him from losing control of the aircraft.

As I explained earlier, it could get very intense in the AC-47 firing pattern. We were flying in the dark of night, around a two-million-candle-power flare, which was also putting out copious amounts of smoke, in a thirty-degree bank and firing from one to three mini-gun machine guns at the enemy. An enemy, who may or may not be firing back at us. As you can see, it would be very easy for the pilot doing the shooting to lose his concentration on flying the aircraft. That is why the copilot was there.

That was my last night to fly with Stubitts. I believe he went home soon after that mission. I developed a new respect for him after that night. The guy was okay in my book.

It was during these two missions with Stubitts that I remembered something I promised myself when I was twelve years old. The promise had to do with the old Tarzan and other Jungle movies I watched back then. In almost every one of them a planeload of people would crash land in the jungle. Invariably, the aircraft they were flying was a C-47. Cannibals, huge snakes, or lions and tigers always ate the people, who were lucky enough to survive the crash. I was smart enough, even at that young age, to say, "You will never catch my ass over a jungle in a C-47." And now, just a mere fifteen years later, here I was in a C-47 over the most hostile jungle in the entire world. In addition to the lions and tigers, that were ready to eat me, there were people down there on the ground trying to shoot me down so they could. This was another one of those ironies of my Vietnam tour.

It had taken me a while, but I was starting to settle into somewhat of a routine there at Nha Trang. I would fly either the early or the late mission.   I preferred the early one because we landed at midnight. The second flight landed at daybreak. I could get my sleeping better regulated when I was able to get to bed around 0100.

After either mission I always went to the Officer's Club for breakfast. It didn't matter if it was midnight or dawn. I usually ordered the same thing every time. I liked chipped beef on toast with a couple of eggs over easy on top. Military slang for chipped beef on toast was SOS or shit on a shingle, but it was a hearty and delicious breakfast.

I would go to my room, get out of my flight suit, go take a shower, and hit the rack. If I were lucky I would sleep six or seven hours. That was easy when I got to bed at 0100. But when I got to bed at 0600 it was a different story. I would sleep sporadically all morning and finally give up around noon. The daytime noise made solid sleep impossible. If I had another flight the next night I would try to supplement my sleep with an afternoon nap. Fortunately I didn't have any extra duties to keep me from doing that.

On nights that I didn't fly, I would hang out at the O Club Bar. On one of my first nights there I noticed a guy sitting alone at the bar. Nobody was sitting next to him. In fact, the other pilots were ignoring him. They acted like he wasn't even there. It was one of the most blatant cases of shunning I have ever seen. I asked one of the pilots with me about him.

"Oh, that piece of shit coward is going home in a few days. He was flying the AC-47 and things got a little too hot for him, so he turned in his wings. His excuse for doing that was 'Fear of Flying'! The son of a bitch had a fear of dying in this war. We are better off without him."

I felt a tinge of pity for the guy, but I knew better than to go speak to him. That would have been the wrong thing to do considering the way the other pilots felt about him. They knew him and I didn't, so I left well enough alone.

Flight Log: June 17, 1969
Spooky 42 Cap Left Seat
Aircraft Commander: Major Reeder
Total time: 4+00   0 Rounds 0 Flares

Major Reeder was an Instructor Pilot, so he invited me to fly left seat on this mission. Unfortunately we didn't get called in for any kind of action this night. We just bored holes in the sky for four hours. But that put me four hours closer to getting in the left seat permanently!

Flight Log: June 18, 1969

Spooky 42   TIC South of Phan Rang   Left Seat
AC / IP: Lieutenant Colonel Hunt
Total time: 4+0 20,667 Rounds 34 Flares

Colonel Hunt was also an Instructor Pilot, so he let me have the left seat again. This time we did get some action and I got to fire my first shot of the war!

A ROK (Republic of South Korea) Unit was caught in a firefight. We came in and set up our firing pattern. I noticed it was very difficult to hold the sight on the target all the way around the circle, so I asked the navigator how strong the winds were at our altitude. He said they were forty-five knots out of the north. Because of this we were able to hold the target only part of the way around, and then I would have to pull off and set up again.

I guess the ROKs got a little impatient with us because in a few minutes we noticed some explosions on the ground all around our position. I looked at Colonel Hunt, he looked at me, and we both said, "Artillery! Those bastards have called artillery in on top of us!"

That meant the shells had to be falling right through our position, and it was just dumb blind luck none of them had blown us out of the sky.

I flew us out of the area and we called the DASC (Direct Air Support Center). We told them what happened and they pulled us off the target. Colonel Hunt just happened to be the Squadron Safety Officer and boy was he pissed off. I think he had the Korean commander on the phone five minutes after we landed.

Flight Log: June 23, 1969

Spooky 42   TIC   Left Seat
AC / IP: Major Longhenry
Total time: 3+50   8500 Rounds 32 Flares

This was another left seat ride for me. It was beginning to look like the Flight leaders were working me into the Aircraft Commander program a little early. I was all for that.

This was a brief firefight. We spent quite a while illuminating the area looking for the enemy. When we located them it didn't take long to eliminate them. The KBA for this mission was ten.

Flight Log: June 26 1969
Spooky 42   TIC Ban Me Tout
Aircraft Commander: Lt Col Bob Davidson
Total time: 4+00   6000 Rounds   32 Flares

This night I would meet a legend in AC-47 lore. His name was Bob Davidson, and he was also known as "Death Valley Dave." Bob was about forty-five years old and I am pretty sure he was single. I assumed that because this was his THIRD straight tour in Vietnam, and all of them in the AC-47. He kept volunteering to stay for another year. Bob had fired more rounds than anyone in the Spooky program, and probably more rounds than anyone in the entire war. I believe it was over two million rounds.

His KBA was unbelievable. He hurt the enemy so badly that they put a bounty of $50,000 on his head. Unfortunately, if you flew with him long enough, they put a bounty on your head too.

Ban Me Thout had a quaint nickname amongst the

troops. They called it "Bang my twat!" My geographic memory is getting a little dull, but I believe Ban Me Thout was near the Cambodian border. We had to fly clear across the country and over the central highlands to get there. Bob must have been very effective that night, because he only needed 6000 rounds to get the job done. I had the bad luck of getting to fly three more times with him. That got me a bounty on my head too!

Flight Log: June 27 1969
Spooky 42   Routine Cap Mission
Aircraft Commander: Lt Col Bob Davidson
Total time: 4+30   0 Rounds 0 Flares

This turned out to be a routine Airborne Alert mission. We didn't see any action that night, and it just about drove Davidson crazy.

"Shit, this is like airline flying! What fun is that?"

"Well Colonel, when the paycheck hits your bank account it can be a lot of fun!" I don't think he cared for that comment.

Flight Log: June 28, 1969
Spooky 41   H&I Mission   Left Seat
AC / IP: Major Berkstead
Total time: 3+54   4000 Rounds 4 Flares

Another left seat ride for me and I was starting to feel better about the program. Even though I didn't have my own crew yet, I was getting to fly the left seat and do the shooting.

That was valuable experience for me. Tonight was just a harassment and interdiction mission. More monkeys and coconuts bit the dust.

I don't remember doing anything special on the fourth of July that year. I do remember thinking about my Dad and being a little sad that I could not call him and wish him a happy birthday. This was the first time in my life that I could not do that. I did make a tape for him that day. He probably got it ten days later.

Speaking of communications with the family, I either wrote a letter or made a tape to Sheila every day. Sometimes I wrote her several times a day. Mail from Vietnam to the United States was free. All you had to do was write the word FREE on the upper right hand corner of the envelope, where the stamp would normally be and it would go through no problem. I wrote Mom and Dad almost as often as I wrote Sheila.

The tapes were nice because I could talk to Theresa. I kept those tapes for a long time, but I stored them in the wrong place and the heat ruined them.

I probably wrote fifteen hundred letters to Sheila during that year. She didn't write that many back but she did write me just about every day. I look at the computer capability we have these days. Oh how nice it would have been to have email and instant messages back then.

One of my major disappointments was the lack of communication I received from people back home. I don't know why, but nobody wrote me over there. The only letters I got were from Sheila, my parents, and her parents. It was a pretty lonely and abandoned feeling, if you ask me. Sometimes it made me wonder for whom I was fighting and if my efforts were even recognized, much less appreciated. I had a lot to learn about the way people back home felt about this war I was fighting.

Flight Log: July 6 & 7, 1969
Ferry Flight to Udorn, Thailand
AC : Lt. Glen "Tiny" Lund
Total time: 9+20

We had a Spooky Flight in Udorn, and Glen Lund and I ferried an airplane to them to use that night. It was a nice daytime flight, and my first trip out of Vietnam since I got there. We spent the night in Udorn and flew back the next day.

Glen was the youngest Aircraft Commander in our Flight. He joined the Flight about six months before I did. He was right out of Undergraduate Pilot Training and this was his first assignment. He had not been an AC long when we flew together, but he did a nice job.

I didn't run into anyone I knew in Udorn, which surprised me, because I always knew somebody every place I went.

Flight Log: July 8, 1969
Local Flight   Day Gunnery Practice　　　　*Left Seat*
AC / IP: Lou Longhenry
Total time: 2+50   6000 Rounds

Major Longhenry took me out over the South China Sea for some day gunnery practice. We dropped a four by four foot float and shot at it. This was the same kind of exercise we did when I was training in Alexandria. I blew the target out of the water!

Flight Log: July 9, 1969
Spooky 41   TIC Mission   Left Seat
AC / IP: Lt Col Rod Wood
Total time: 4+10   10,000 Rounds 17 Flares

Maybe they were not able to let me have my own crew until I reached the "magic" two hundred hours, but they were giving me a lot of time in the left seat. I appreciated that very much.

We were called out for a troops-in-contact mission this night. I don't remember where it was or how many KBA's we had.

I flew left seat rides number 8 through 12 with colonel Woods. Two were CAP missions and three were Troops in Contact. We fired 25,000 rounds and expended 17 flares.

Flight Log: July 21, 1969 (Moon Landing)
Spooky 42   H&I Mission   Left Seat
AC / IP: Major Lou Longhenry
Total time: 3+10   10,000 Rounds 0 Flares

This was another H & I mission. If the date sounds familiar is should. This was the night Neil Armstrong and Buzz Aldrin landed on the Moon!

I was in the middle of shooting up a free fire area. The target was so open there we didn't even have to drop flares to identify it. The navigator interrupted me and said, "Hey

Mike, monitor Fox Mike 2!" That meant he wanted me to listen to FM Radio #2. I opened my switch and I heard the NASA controller talking to the moon lander. They were just about to touch down. I rolled wings level, ordered gun's cold, and told the crew to listen to the radio. I said, "Men, the first manned moon landing happens only once. Let's listen to it. The war can wait a few minutes."

It was pretty surreal flying there in the oldest airplane in the Air Force inventory, listening to our guys landing on the moon! As soon as they were safely down, I rolled back into the firing pattern and ordered "guns hot!"

Flight Log: July 23, 1969
Spooky 42   H&I Mission
AC: Venable Hammonds
Total time: 4+10   6,000 Rounds 10 Flares

This ride was Lt. Venable Hammond's first flight as Aircraft Commander. It was just another H&I mission, but "Ven" did a great job. He flew that left seat like he had been doing it all his life. I was happy to be with him on this special flight in his career.

Flight Log: July 27, 1969
Local Flight – Functional Check Flight   Left Seat
AC: Lt Colonel Rod Wood
Total time: 0+20

Ship number 686 had an engine change and Col Wood

called me and said he wanted me to go on the Maintenance check flight with him. It was a short flight. All we had to do was takeoff, climb to 3000 feet, shut down the new engine, feather the prop, and then unfeather it and start it back up. The whole thing took twenty minutes, but it was a good experience for me. It was actually the first time I had feathered a propeller on the C-47. I flew another left seat mission with Col Wood on August 1. It was just an Airborne Alert flight.

Flight Log: August 3, 1969
Spooky 42 Scramble TIC Mission Left Seat
AC: Col Rod Wood
Total time: 4+10 6,000 Rounds 24 Flares

We were scrambled on a TIC mission. When we got to the target area things had quieted down. The ground commander gave us a target area and said, "Shoot over there and see if you can stir them up!"

I rolled in on the target and was just about to squeeze the trigger when suddenly, right in the center of my gun site, was the flash of ground fire. It could not have been more perfectly aligned.

I told Col Wood what I saw. "That unlucky son of a bitch. He just picked the wrong time to take a potshot at an airplane."

I gave the trigger a one second squeeze and sent one hundred rounds of 7.62 ammo back at him. We must have hit them where they hurt, because the whole mountainside lit up.

We were able to suppress all that fire and make everything quiet pretty quickly. I know I killed a lot of people over there, but this one guy who was in my gun-site, stays in my memory. I flew with Wood again the next night, and Lund two nights later. Both were H&I missions.

Flight Log: August 9, 1969
Spooky 41   TIC   Navy Gun Boat "Mustang"
IP: Major Lou Longhenry
Time: 4+20   21,000 Rounds 22 Flares
Time: 1+00   21,000 Rounds 24 Flares
Time: 1+24   21,000 Rounds 22 Flares
Total: 6+44 63,000 Rounds 68 Flares

This was one of the wildest missions of my entire tour in the AC-47. We were flying airborne patrol just off the coast at Nha Trang and we were passing an inlet made by the mainland and a hilly peninsula that jutted out into the South China Sea. I looked down and saw an unusual sight. Tracers were going from the water to the shore and from the shore to the water.

I told the navigator to start sweeping the FM radio bands to see if anyone was calling. In a couple of seconds we heard, "This is Mustang, we are a riverboat and we are trapped in an inlet off Nha Trang. Request air support!"

I picked up my microphone and said, "Mustang, this is Spooky 41. We are directly over the top of you. How can we help you tonight?"

"Spooky, so glad to see you! We have a shitload of bad guys on the hillside north of us. We caught them unloading a bunch of stuff on the shoreline, but we don't have enough firepower to deal with them, and now we are trapped in this inlet."

"Well, I think we have all the firepower you will need! If you will be so kind as to point them out with your tracers, we will take care of the rest. Let me get into firing position and I'll give you the signal to mark the target."

He replied, "Roger that Spooky!"

The hill on the peninsula was steep, so making our standard left turn firing circle was not going to work. That would have taken us too close to the ground, where ground fire would have been a real threat. There was also the possibility of running into the hill by turning toward it.

I talked it over with Lou and said, "How about making right turns to get into position for a lateral strafing run along the peninsula, instead of trying to make this a circular pattern?" He agreed that would be a good solution.

I relayed my intentions to Mustang and when I was lined up for firing pass.

"Okay Mustang, mark the target."

He fired some tracers into the hillside and I followed them up with one gun at fast rate of fire. The entire hillside erupted in gunfire. There must have been at least two or three hundred bad guys down there. When I reached the end of the peninsula I made a steep right turn to get back in position.

On this run I told Mustang I was going to strafe the shoreline to see if they had left any explosives or petrol there. He concurred. I lined up again and this time strafed the entire shoreline of the peninsula. About halfway down, and just opposite of where Mustang was, all hell broke loose. We were getting secondary explosions all over the beach. Apparently this was a major resupply effort on the part of the enemy.

We made three more firing passes and we were still getting resistance. I told Mustang we were running out of ammo
and that we needed to land and reload. I said we were based
right there at Nha Trang and would be back in less than
twenty minutes. He said he thought he could hold on until
then. We called the base and told them we needed a rapid
reload of flares and bullets. We were okay on fuel. I have to
give my crew great credit here, because they worked their
butts off to get us reloaded. We were airborne again in ten
minutes and back on the target in fifteen.

We kept making strafing runs along the hill until we ran
out of flares and ammo again. We landed a second time and
reloaded. It was getting close to daybreak now. When we
were back on station I told Mustang this was going to have
to be it. I wanted him to get ready to make his break for open
water. I would tell him when to go.

I came back around and when I was in position to start
my run I told Mustang to gun it and get out of there. As I
made my pass I fired all three guns at full rate of fire. I
wagged my wings, as one would wag a garden hose to water
a lawn, and saturated the entire hillside with 18,000 rounds
per minute,. There was no way anyone on the ground was
going to be able to shoot back with all that covering fire-
power coming at them.

As I finished the firing run Mustang called and said,
"Thanks Spooky! We are in the clear in open water!"

"That's a good deal Mustang, because I shot my entire
wad on that last pass." About that time I looked up and saw
a C-119 "Shadow" Gunship coming on station.

"Hey Spooky, Shadow 42 here. Understand you have an
empty quiver. We'll clean up here for you. Great work

buddy!"

At our intelligence briefing the next day we learned that our KBA was over 200 and we had stopped a major resupply operation the Vietcong were running. They were planning to attack Nha Trang with those munitions we blew up! I fired 63,000 rounds into that hillside that night! That was the night that the Intelligence Officer gave me the nickname "Trigger Trahan!" It looked like I was becoming the heir apparent to "Death Valley Dave."

Our mission made the front page of The Air Force Times newspaper, and that was nice, but the main thing was this – four Navy gunboat crewmen were alive because of what we did that night. The entire crew of Spooky 41 was nominated for The Distinguished Cross for that mission.

This is a side note, but I have to mention it here. It was forty-seven years later, and one day I was on Facebook and I had posted this short story about the Spooky/Mustang mission for my Facebook Friends. I little while later I got a message from Billy Clark.

"Mike, I was your Flight Engineer on that mission!"

I had not seen or heard from any of my Spooky Brothers since the war, and this encounter with Billy led me back to them. We went to a Spooky reunion that same year.

Flight Log: August 10, 1969
Spooky 41   TIC Mission
AC: Lt Colonel Bob Davidson
Total time: 1.4   0 Rounds 24 Flares

Things were starting to heat up in the war. I had flown nearly seven hours during the night and early morning of

August 9 & 10, and here I was airborne less than twelve hours later.

We were flying airborne alert again and Bob decided to fly over Cam Ranh Bay and check it out. When we arrived we noticed some activity on the beach outside the base. It looked like mortar flashes to us. We called Cam Ranh Bay tower and asked if anything was going on down there.

"Yeah Spooky, we just took some mortar rounds."

Bob told the loadmaster to throw out a flare and as soon as it lit we saw a bunch of bad guys on the beach. There must have been at least fifty of them.

Bob yelled, "Gun's hot! I'm gonna kill these bastards!"

The navigator said, "Bob, we don't have clearance to fire yet. I am talking to our DASC (Direct Air Support Center) right now. They are trying to locate the Vietnamese province chief to get permission to shoot in that area."

Bob was livid, and so was I. We could have ended that attack with a two second burst of fire, but we never fired a shot that night. Clearance to fire came thirty minutes later, and by then it was too late. Those same guys who were lobbing the mortars into the base also went into the base hospital and threw some satchel charges around. They killed several of our wounded GI's there in the hospital.

We had to land to reload flares, and we were supposed to go back up and finish our Cap Mission, but Bob was so upset he said, "Screw this shit. I'm not going back up tonight. We can spend the rest of our alert on the ground. If the son of a bitches won't let us shoot, why the hell even be up there?"

I was right with him in those sentiments.

I had just one more flight with "Death Valley Dave" and

I was glad of it. That man was so intense and, after three tours, he had just about beaten all the odds he was going to beat. His number had to be close to coming up and I didn't want to be up there with him when it did. We went up on our last flight together the following night.

Flight Log: August 11, 1969
Spooky 41   TIC Mission
AC: Lt Colonel Bob Davidson
Total time: 3+10   21,000   Rounds 17 Flares

We had just gotten airborne when we got a call that there were some troops in contact near Phan Re. As I recall, Phan Re was nestled up close to some pretty rugged high terrain. The navigator looked at the coordinates of the target and said, "Bob, this is going to be a dicey one. This place is in a blind valley right up against the mountains. We are going to have to go through a small opening to get in and out of there, and we are not going to have a lot of room to maneuver once in there. Please trust and fly the headings I give you. It's the only way we are going to get in and out of there without splattering our asses on this mountain." Bob said he would.

This was one of the scariest missions of the entire war for me. We flew through that opening, which was about a mile wide, and into an enclosed valley that was about six miles wide and four miles deep. There were hills above and all around us. We threw out a flare and located the enemy, using directions from our friendly forces down there. Once Bob got into his firing pattern he was so focused on that he forgot about the airplane. I caught him at sixty and seventy degrees of bank several times. I had to yell at him to fly the airplane first.

Everyone was focused on the target and I seemed to be the only one interested in the terrain around us. Those hills loomed large right outside my window. At times it looked like we were awfully close to them. When you added the brightness and smoke from the flares and the tracers and noise from the guns, it became a bizarre scene. I'll admit I did some praying that night.

We expended all our ammunition and most of our flares, but Bob had ended the attack. The good guys said the bad guys were all dead or gone. I was so glad when we went back through our little opening and into more hospitable terrain.

One reason I was a little shaky up in those mountains was this. Just the week before we got word that one of our AC-47s out of Tan Son Nhut had flown into the only mountain near Saigon and killed the entire crew. That was pretty heavy on my mind as those hills whizzed by my window this night.

When we landed Bob said, "You did a great job Mike. Thanks for keeping the airplane upright tonight. Sometimes I get a little carried away." Then he did something I'll never forget. He slapped me on the back and said, like a coach who was overjoyed about a football victory, "We killed them tonight Mike! We KILLED them!"

Old Bob had been there too long. He was going home soon and I knew I would not fly with him again. I was glad I had the opportunity to fly with him some but I was also glad I didn't have to do it any more.

Someone once told me that courage was, "When you are scared to death and you are the only one who knows it!" I agree with that to the extent that it is something a leader, especially an aircraft commander, must be able to do. You must exhibit confidence in all situations or it undermines the confidence of your crew. And you must be able to do that even if your confidence level is low.

Flying is inherently dangerous and combat flying even more so. If you are flying combat missions, day after day, and you are not experiencing any fear, then there is something seriously wrong with you or you just don't understand the situation. Was I afraid over there at times? You bet your ass I was!

I think true courage is experiencing great fear and then overcoming that fear and going out and doing your job in spite of it, sometimes over and over again! There was always a certain amount of anxiety and uncertainty before every mission. Sometimes, depending on the intelligence reports, that anxiety level could be very high.

I can only relate it to how we used to feel before the first kickoff in a football game. We would be tense and there would be some fear, but once we kicked off and made that first hit, the fear disappeared and the game was on! I had that same experience while flying the AC-47. I would approach every target with some anxiety and uncertainty, but once I rolled in and started shooting all that went away and I became what I was there to be – an effective aggressive combat pilot.

Someone once asked me what it was like being in Vietnam for a year. They said, "What emotions did you experience Mike?" I told them I experienced four major emotions and they alternated in priority depending on the situation I found myself in at the time. Those emotions were - excited, lonely, horny, or scared!

Flight Log: August 16 & 17, 1969
Special Mission – Pick up Aircraft from Taiwan
AC: Lt Glen "Tiny" Lund
Taipei to Hong Kong - Total time: 5+00
Hong Kong to Nha Trang – Total time: 4+15

This was one of those good deal trips. Glen Lund and I

were picked to go get an airplane that had been in Taipei, Taiwan for IRAN (Inspection and Repairs as Necessary). We took two navigators and a flight engineer and caught a C-130 to Taipei on August 15. The next day we picked up an airplane and flew it to Hong Kong. Hong Kong was just a stopping point along the way, but gosh what an exotic stopping point it was! I was fascinated by that city.

There was something nostalgic and even romantic about flying an old C-47 over those waters. I felt like we were a throwback to the 1940's when airplanes like that were all over the skies over there. It was just a cool feeling.

Our approach into Hong Kong was interesting. We had to fly into a big inlet waterway towards some mountains. There were a series of turns before you could line up with the runway. To indicate where to turn there were big checkerboards placed on the side of the mountains. You would fly to this checkerboard and turn right and then fly to the next one and turn right again. The next thing you knew there was the runway in front of you. Making those turns was a piece of cake in the C-47, because that approach was designed for that airplane. However, doing it in a modern jet is another story and requires a lot more skill and planning.

We spent the afternoon and evening in Hong Kong. Someone in Taiwan gave us the name and address of a custom tailor in Hong Kong and somehow we found him. I had a suit and four custom shirts made. I think the total bill was $100 including shipping!

The next day we flew nonstop from Hong Kong back to Nha Trang. It was a nice trip and it was so good to be out of the war zone for at least a couple of days.

My long-suffering days in the right seat were coming to

an end. I flew one more copilot mission with Lund on August 19 and a couple of left seat flights with Major Longhenry on august 20 and 21.

On August 22 I flew to Pleiku and Danang with Captain Phil Greeley. Phil was a flight examiner so I flew left seat on this trip. On the 23rd we flew back to Nha Trang. Phil said I was ready for my Aircraft Commander Check Ride. He set it up for August 25.

Flight Log: August 25, 1969
Aircraft Commander – Daytime Proficiency Check
AC: Captain Phil Greeley
Total time: 1+ 15

Phil took me out over the water and we did approaches to stalls, steep turns, and some other maneuvers. Then we went to Cam Ranh Bay and did our pattern work. On my last approach he pulled the engine back and said, "Engine Failure." He intended for me to land out of it and instead I went around. I don't know why I did that but Phil was pleased with my go around procedure. He laughed and said, "You made this harder than it needed to be. You did a nice job Mike. I'm sorry you had to wait so long to get to be an AC over here. What a damn waste of talent putting you in the copilot seat so long."

I thanked him and said, "Don't worry about it Phil. I'm used to that!"

Flight Log: August 27, 1969 - Spooky 41

Aircraft Commander – Tactical Check Ride
AC: Major Crider
Total time: 5+55   17,000 Rounds 3 Flares

This was a troops in contact mission and it was a pretty dicey one at that. We were called in to help a unit that was about to be overrun and the enemy was mere yards away from our guys. They gave us their position and asked us to fire within fifty yards of a fence line they pointed out. They were on one side of the fence and the bad guys on the other.

I carefully laced in some fire and asked them how that was working. They came back and said it was fine, but to come a little bit closer. I did.

And then came the most dreaded call a pilot can hear, "Stop firing Spooky, I think we have a friendly out in the fire zone!" Sure enough, there was a South Vietnamese army guy on the wrong side of the fence. He had gotten under a log and had a scratch on his elbow. Fortunately we were not charged with a "Short Round" which is a round that didn't hit its intended target, and instead hit a friendly. None of my rounds hit anywhere but in the designated target area.

I don't remember our KBA for that night because when I landed I had to spend a couple of hours filling out paperwork. And oh, by the way, I passed my Tactical Check Ride for Spooky Aircraft Commander.

I was sitting at the bar in the Officer's Club one night. I had my back to the room, which was unusual for me. Suddenly there were a couple of massive arms wrapped around me and some big guy had me in a bear hug. A voice said, "Duke, what the hell are you doing here?"

Only someone who knew me at Ole Miss would know about that nickname. I got that in practice when Coach Vought complimented me for a good run. I said, "Coach, just call me Duke, because nothing could stop the Duke of Earle!" The guy hugging me was Jamie Ray Little! Jamie Ray got to Ole Miss in my sophomore year. He had been assigned to A Flight and was just reporting in.

Jamie had been flying EC-135s in the Strategic Air Command before getting his Vietnam orders. Somehow he heard I was at Nha Trang. I was delighted he was going to be in the flight with us.

With Ole Miss teammate Jamie Ray Little

Flight Log: August 27, 1969 - Armstrong's Last Flight
Spooky 41   TIC Mission
AC: Lt Colonel Ben Armstrong
Total time: 2+20   14,500 Rounds 17 Flares

Ben got some action on his last flight. We were called to a location along a road north of Nha Trang. A convoy had been ambushed. Ben was able to put a stop to that in short order. We had a good time together on his last mission. He said he would be around another couple of weeks, but he was finished flying. He told me he was getting out of the Air Force as soon as he got back to the United States, and that he was moving to Pretoria, South Africa.

Flight Log: September 6, 1969
Daylight Cross Country   Nha Trang to Pleiku
AC: Captain Mike Trahan
Total time: 1+40   Nha Trang to Pleiku
Total time: 3+ 45   Pleiku to Nha Trang

My first Aircraft Commander flight was a parts run to Pleiku. One of our squadron aircraft needed a critical part so I was asked to fly it up there. Lt. Richard Opdyke was my copilot and Sergeants Basher and Perkins came along too. I had flown into Pleiku once in the C-141 and I remembered a little bit about it. One thing I especially remembered was that Pleiku was always surrounded on all sides by enemy troops. There was no safe place to crash land an airplane outside the perimeter of that base.

The other memorable thing about Pleiku was a land-mark about ten miles south of the base. We flew right over it on our flight up there. It was a little hill and the only way I can describe it accurately was that it looked just exactly like a woman's vagina! Of course the nickname of that hill was "Pussy Mountain" and of course it had to be one of the most used reporting points in Vietnam. It was famous all over the country.

We dropped off the part and headed back to Nha Trang. We took twice as long to get back to Nha Trang because we had to divert around some thunderstorms.

For some reason I was not flying combat missions during this period. I don't think anyone was. We had lulls like this from time to time over there. Most of my flying was daylight flights to different bases delivering parts and people. We had a couple of C-47's that were configured as passenger / cargo aircraft. We used those for these flights.

On September 7 I flew a functional check flight with Major Lazrus. He was getting close to going home and he wanted a highly experienced pilot in the right seat for this flight.

Flight Log: September 8, 1969
Daylight Cross Country   NORS Run
AC: Captain Mike Trahan
Total time: 8+30

This flight was something new. I don't know if it was because we were not doing much fighting at the time or if it was the bright idea of someone up in Wing Headquarters, but suddenly we were running a parts delivery service. NORS means an aircraft or some piece of equipment was "not on ready status." The parts that were necessary to put them back on ready status were classified as "NORS" parts.

We hit nine bases all over South Vietnam that day. It was a very interesting flight from the geographical aspect of it. We got a great tour of the country.

Flight Log: September 9, 1969
Daylight Cross Country   Special Flight
AC: Captain Mike Trahan

Total time: 2+30

This was one of the most unusual flights of the year. I was told to take the cargo version of the C-47 and fly it to Saigon Tan San Nhut air base.

We parked at Base Operations as instructed and they started loading ceramic elephants on our airplane. There were twenty of them and they were all about three feet tall, two feet wide, and four feet long. A Lieutenant Colonel was supervising the loading and I walked over to him. In my war weary voice I said, "Colonel, what the hell is this shit?"

"Captain, that information does not fall under your need to know. Just fly this load to Nha Trang and don't ask any more questions about it."

"Yes sir!"

After we were loaded and the cargo tied down carefully with nets, an armed courier boarded the airplane. He was our only passenger and this was our only cargo.

"Will you be able to explain this to me after we land in Nha Trang?" I asked.

He replied, "Yes sir. And I will do that."

We made it back to Nha Trang with all the elephants intact. Once they were loaded in armored cars I started to figure it out. The courier came over and I said, "We are carrying greenbacks aren't we?"

"Yes sir, about three million dollars worth!"

"Well hell man, why didn't you tell me that on the way here? We could have made a right turn and flown to Singapore."

"Yes sir, and that's why I didn't tell you. I might have been tempted to go along with it."

We both laughed.

Our Operations Officer, Major Longhenry, was finishing his tour in a couple of weeks and would be going home. There was some speculation about who would take his place. Our Flight Commander, Lt. Colonel Rod Wood, was also leaving soon. I think he had just a month to go.

One night Jamie Little, some of the lieutenants in the flight, and I were sitting at a table in the Officer Club bar. We were talking about the upcoming vacancies at the top of our Flight. I had been imbibing a little bit and had just enough "liquid courage" to make an outrageous statement that was loud enough to be heard by anyone within ten feet of our table.

"Hell, if I could have Jamie as my Operations Officer and you guys as my Aircraft Commanders I believe I could run our flight as well as those Old Fart Colonels are running their flights. And I think we could have the best damn flight in the Squadron!"

About that time I felt a tap on my shoulder. It was Colonel Armstrong, the Squadron Operations Officer.

Captain Trahan, report to my office at 0800 tomorrow!"

I had actually made a pretty bold statement that night. All five Flight Commanders in the 4th Special Operations Squadron were Lieutenant Colonels. It was audacious of me to put myself on a par with people of that kind of rank, but I still felt I could handle the job.

When I walked into Colonel Armstrong's office the next morning I was surprised to see the Squadron and D Flight Commanders sitting there. Colonel Swigler spoke first, "Well Captain Trahan, I hear you think you can run D Flight as well as any of us old fart Lieutenant Colonels. Do you really feel that way?"

"Well sir, I was popping off a little bit, and I certainly meant no disrespect when I called you all Old Fart LC's, but to answer your question, yes sir, I do believe I could run this flight."

"That's all we needed to hear Mike. We wanted to be sure you had the balls for it and the desire to do it. You've got the job!"

Man, you could have knocked me over with a feather.

"Sir, are you serious? Is this for real?"

"Yes, we had already decided to make you D Flight Commander when Colonel Woods leaves. You are not the highest ranked officer we have, but you are the most experienced AC-47 pilot in this flight, and you have exhibited excellent leadership skills. We are confident you will do a good job for us. Major Longhenry is leaving in two weeks. Starting today you are the Operations Officer of D Flight. Major Longhenry will familiarize you with every aspect of the operations of this flight. After he leaves you will be mentored by Colonel Wood on the job of running the flight. Congratulations!"

I thanked them and then I said, "Can I pick my own Operations Officer and Aircraft Commanders?" They said I could.

"Very well then. I am your man. Thank you for your confidence. I will do my best to make you happy with this decision you have made."

They laughed and Armstrong said, "We are already happy with it Mike!"

Major Longhenry spent the rest of the day getting me up

to speed on scheduling, training, and qualifications require-ments for the flight. I told him about my experience in the Squadron Training Office in Charleston and he said that was excellent preparation for this job. I told him I had chosen Jamie Little as my Operations Officer and he said to tell Jamie to come in and learn this job with me, since he was the one who would be taking it over.

When I got off that evening I sent word to Sergeant George Dowling that I wanted to see him. I asked him to meet me in my room. George was the most senior Non-Com-missioned Officer in the Flight, and he was the direct super-visor of all the enlisted men in the Flight. He would report directly to me.

When he got to my room I poured us both a stiff drink and said, "Well George, I may have let my mouth overload my ass!"

"Yes Sir, I heard you were going to be our next Flight Commander!" I was surprised to hear him saying that, be-cause the announcement had not been made. He knew any-way. Never underestimate the resourcefulness of a senior NCO!

"George, I asked you to come by tonight because I am going to need your help running this flight. I know how to deal with officers, but I don't have a clue how to work with enlisted men. I am going to leave that up to you. Can I count on you to take care of that end of it for me?"

"Yes Sir, I can and I will be happy to. Can I count on your support too?"

"Of course you can!" We shook hands and I never had to spend a minute worrying about the enlisted men.

Master Sergeant George Dowling

A couple of days later we had a Squadron meeting and my promotion to Flight Commander was announced. It was well received by the members of D Flight, both the officers and the enlisted men. There were a couple of Majors in the flight who were not pleased because they were passed over for the job, but they were both new to the squadron and were just not familiar enough with our combat operations to handle the job.

Chapter 15

We Move The Flight To Phan Rang

I was in for another major surprise the next time I went into the office. Colonel Swigler told me my first job as Flight Commander was to move the entire flight from Nha Trang to Phan Rang!

I asked him what kind of time frame we were talking about and he said, "The move will be complete by October 1!" That was just two weeks away!

We had to immediately set up a series of shuttle flights from Nha Trang to Phan Rang to get our office equipment moved down there. Fortunately our combat sortie commitment was cut so we could accomplish this move. For the next two weeks we ran these shuttles twice a day. We use C-123's and C-130's to move our larger heavier equipment.

Flight Log: September 21 & 22, 1969
Spooky 41   Troops In Contact
Spooky 41   Regenerate   TIC
AC: Captain Mike Trahan
Time: 2+00   16,500 Rounds 22 Flares
Time: 3+15   21,000 Rounds 24 Flares

Just about the time we were busiest with our move to Phan Rang the war heated up. I had to pull double duty this night. On our first alert shift we scrambled to a TIC near the base. It was another Navy gunboat needing help. The Navy guys had discovered a big materiel drop off and caught the bad guys by surprise. They just didn't have enough fire-power to do the job. We came in and blew up everything on that beach. I don't care what anyone says, getting secondary explosions from your gunfire is exciting! We got a lot of secondary explosions that night. We also took a lot of ground fire back at us.

After we finished there we went back to Nha Trang and reloaded. We still had three more hours of alert time to pull. We had no sooner gotten in bed when we were scrambled again. This time the target was inland and it was another troops in contact. Apparently there was a big move afoot this night, because we destroyed another stockpile of fuel and ammunition on this mission too. I never got as many secondary explosions as I got this night.

For the next week we did nothing but shuttle men and equipment to Phan Rang. I would fly the morning mission from Nha Trang to Phan Rang, carrying another Aircraft Commander with me. He would fly the airplane back to Nha Trang and I would stay in Phan Rang and set up my Flight Offices. Then I would fly home on the evening shuttle.

I liked the facilities at Phan Rang. The base was consid-erably more inland than Nha Trang, which was right on the coast. Housing was a little short there though, and some of us had to share a room. Jamie Little and I were roommates! We were teammates at Ole Miss and four years later we were roommates in Viet Nam.

Before we leave Nha Trang, I would like to tell you one little story about it. It didn't involve flying. It involved recre-ation!

Nha Trang city was nestled along a crescent beach that could rival any beach in the world. The sand was as white as the sand in Pensacola Florida and the water was crystal clear. One time a bunch of us went out on a boat and did some snorkeling. The water was about forty feet where we got out of the boat and when I put my facemask in the water I got the sudden sense that I was flying, and that there was nothing between the bottom and me. A short distance away there was a reef and the water was eight to ten feet deep there. The reef was teeming with fish and lobsters. We caught enough lobsters to have a feast that night.

There was one incident, however, that really put a damper on the day for us. We had gone around a corner on a peninsula and were out of sigh of the mainland. About that time a boat came racing up, and the men on it were shooting guns. We thought they were shooting at us but they weren't. They were some South Korean soldiers messing with us. If they had been a boatload of Viet Cong, we would have definitely been captured or killed that day. We did not have any kind of weapons on board to defend ourselves with.

Jamie Little and I worked out a schedule that would divide the workload between us. There was no way I could fly half the night and work all day running the flight, so he and I split the duties. I would fly the first mission of the night and he would take the second. I would take the morning shift at the office and he would take the afternoon. I pretty much had all the scheduling done by the time he got there, but he was there to man the desk in case something came up. He was more like a Co-Flight Commander than an Operations Officer.

To the best of my recollection we had just four Aircraft Commanders left in A Flight by the time we got to Phan Rang. They were Glen Lund, Venable Hammonds, Jamie Little, and myself. We also had some help from the Squadron. Colonel Swigler and Phil Greeley flew with us. We had to staff two flights a night so that meant everyone was flying at least every third night, and in most cases the A Flight pilots were flying every other night. You can see in the picture below how gaunt I had become trying to keep up with a killer schedule like that.

Working on the flight schedule.

Colonel Swigler called me in his office one day and said, "Mike, we are going to have to put you back in the right seat."

I wasn't sure what he meant. "Have I done something wrong, that I am not aware of?"

He laughed and said, "No we need you to upgrade to Instructor Pilot so some of these young lieutenants can get some left seat time. They need the in-country experience just like you did."

"That's fine with me Sir, when do I check out?"

"Phil Greeley will give you your Transition Check tomorrow and your Tactical Check the next night."

And that was that! Two days later I was an AC-47 Instructor Pilot.

Flight Log: October 14, 1969
Local Flight   Instructor Pilot Transition Check Ride
AC/IP: Captain Mike Trahan
Flight Examiner: Phil Greeley
Time: 2+30

Phil took me up and had me instruct him in some maneuvers. Everything went well and I passed the ride.

Flight Log: October 15, 1969
Spooky 41   Instructor Pilot Tactical Check Ride
AC: Captain Mike Trahan
Flight Examiner: Phil Greeley
Time: 5+15   0 Rounds   0 Flares

We didn't get any action on this flight, but Phil signed me off anyway. We spent the entire night talking about what I would do in this or that situation and he was apparently satisfied with my answers. When we landed I was a fully qualified Instructor Pilot.

On October 21 I caught a ride with one of our AC-47's that was heading for Clark AFB in the Philippines. My friends Erv and Pam Prince were based there and I wanted to spend my week of leave time visiting with them. I could not go on R&R and be with Sheila until January, but it was high time I took some time off and got out of Vietnam for a little while. I noticed the date of this trip also happened to be my second wedding anniversary! When I landed in Clark I used the MARS phone and called Sheila to wish her a happy anniversary. She was so surprised to hear from me.

I got a trailer for my quarters while I was at Clark that week. I believe they set those up especially for officers on leave from Vietnam. It was nice enough.

I was able to contact Erv and Pam and they invited me to come over to their apartment off base for dinner. Pam asked me what I wanted and I said, "Pam, can you make chicken fricassee?" She said she could and boy could she! It was delicious. The next night she asked me again what I wanted, and I said, "Chicken Fricassee please!" I asked for the same thing the night after that too. I loved it!

When I got back to Phan Rang on the third of November I learned that my time away was not quite over. Colonel Swigler sent Jim Popovich, a navigator, a flight engineer and me back to Tai Chung, Taiwan to pick up an airplane that was coming out of IRAN. We caught a ride on a C-130 to Tai Chung early on the morning of November 4. We flew to Clark that same day and spent the night. I called Erv and Pam and said I was back and asked her to cook another fricassee so Jim could taste it. She did and he loved it. We flew back to Phan Rang the next day.

When we got back to Phan Rang this time, we learned that the war had heated up considerably. In fact, one of the largest NVA offensives of the war was underway. Approximately five thousand North Vietnamese Army troops were massing in the Parrot's Beak area of Cambodia, just across the Mekong River from Duc Lop and Bhu Prang. Duc Lop and

Bhu Prang were two large ARVIN (Army of South Vietnam) bases and they were in danger of being overrun. I scheduled my favorite copilot, Jim Popovich, to fly with me and away we went.

Flight Log: November 9, 1969
Spooky 42   Engine Problems
AC: Captain Mike Trahan
CP: Lt Jim Popovich
Time: 1+00   0 Rounds 0 Flares

We were fragged (ordered) to fly to the Duc Loc Special Forces camp on the Cambodian Border. That was a pretty long flight and involved crossing the mountains of the central highlands of South Vietnam. One of the dangers of this mission was if we lost an engine over the target we could not make it back to Phan Rang. The airplane would not climb high enough on one engine to clear the mountains. In that case our only option was to fly south down the Mekong River to Saigon. That would have been a treacherous flight.

I had to climb to 10,500 feet to clear the mountains on the way to the target. As we were climbing through 8,500 the right engine started backfiring. It got so bad I had to bring it back to idle power to keep the backfiring from damaging it. I tried twice to bring the power back in and both times the backfiring came back. I could not see bringing an airplane with a faulty engine into a combat situation, so I elected to abort the mission and land at the nearest base, which was Cam Ranh Bay.

We stayed at Cam Rahn Bay until daylight and I elected to fly the airplane back to Phan Rang. On the way down there

I climbed back to 8,000 feet and the engine started backfiring again.

When we got back there all hell broke loose. Colonel Swigler was livid that I aborted a mission. I told him about the backfire and he appeared to be skeptical that the engine was actually doing that. I said, "Sir, please come with me and I will show you."

I asked Sergeant Dowling to go up with us. He was my best Flight Engineer. I got in the left seat, Colonel Swigler got in the right seat. After takeoff I immediately climbed to 8,000 feet. As it had done the previous two times at this altitude, the right engine started backfiring violently. I just kept climbing and the backfiring kept getting worse. The engine was acting like it was trying to tear itself off the wing. I just let it keep on backfiring. Finally Swigler said, "You better shut that engine down or it's going to blow up."

I looked at him and said, "Sir, are you convinced that I was justified in aborting that mission last night?"

He said, "Yes I am." I brought the engine to idle power and kept it there until we were in the traffic pattern.

After we got on the ground I told Colonel Swigler I was very disappointed he questioned my judgment and my motives for aborting that mission.

"You made me you're Alpha Flight Commander and the first time I make a major decision you questioned it in front of my crew. That undermined my credibility with my men Colonel. If you don't trust my judgment maybe I should step down."

He then did something a senior officer seldom does, and I give him great credit for this. He apologized to me. I left his office still Commander of Alpha Flight.

Flight Log: November 10, 1969
Spooky 41   TIC Duc Lop
AC: Captain Mike Trahan
CP: Lt Jim Popovich
Time: 5+00   21,000 Rounds 24 Flares

I scheduled the same men, who were with me when we had the backfiring engine, to fly with me on this mission. I knew it was going to be a hot one and I wanted them to be a part of it.

When we got to Duc Lop all hell was breaking loose. There was an American advisor with the Vietnamese soldiers down there and he was on the radio with us.

"Spooky! Are we ever glad to see you! Our camp is being overrun right now. I'm not sure how many, but there must be hundreds of NVA coming into the camp. We are all bunkered in. I want you to put your fire right on top of us Spooky. It's our only chance."

I made him verify that he wanted me to fire INSIDE the camp area and he repeated it. He said, "Everyone is bunkered in. We are all safe. Get those bastards off of us Spooky and do it now!"

I told the loadmaster to throw out a flare and when it lit we could see people all over that camp. I verified the target with the navigator and confirmed that we were cleared to fire on the camp itself. We were! I called Guns Hot and rolled in on the target. I used all three guns on fast rate and sprayed the hell out of that camp. The guy on the ground was so shook up he forgot to release the transmit button on his radio. We could hear the bullets hitting the ground and the top of his bunker. We could also hear the carnage and chaos that was taking place above that bunker. I completely saturated the camp in less than three minutes of firing. Our ground contact called us back and said, "You can stop firing now Spooky. I think you got them ALL! You guys really saved our butts here tonight. Thank you!"

I told him we were happy to help and glad they were okay. I said we were out of ammunition and that we had to return to base to reload. He said, "Spooky, I don't think we will need your help any more tonight. I just climbed out of the bunker and there are dead Gooks all over this camp. Thank you again."

We landed at Phan Rang and refueled and loaded ammo and flares and took off again to fly Airborne Alert. Spooky 42 had to abort because of mechanical problems, so we took their mission too. We flew over nine hours that night.

We didn't get called on any more targets but we had already done a pretty good night's work. The next day the Intelligence Officer told me our KBA for that mission was estimated at more than 200 killed. We had definitely saved that Special Forces Camp from being overrun and captured and that fact was making its way known all the way up the chain of command. A few months later I got notice that my crew and I were receiving the Vietnamese Cross of Gallantry with Silver Star for that mission.

Flight Log: November 20, 1969
Spooky 41   TIC Bu Prang
AC: Captain Mike Trahan
CP: Lt Jim Popovich
Time: 4+50   100 Rounds 1 Flare

Do you remember when I told you about the guy who fired at me just as I was rolling in on a target, and how he was in the exact center of my gun sight?" Well this mission was even more bizarre.

We were told to fly over to the Cambodian border and provide airborne alert and support for the Vietnamese Special Forces Camp at Bhu Prang. When we arrived over the camp we checked in with them.

The man on the ground said, "Spooky, things are fairly quiet, but we are having problems with a sniper out there in the trees north of camp. The little bastard is taking potshots at anything that moves in the camp. Can you rid us of him for us?"

"We'll do our best, but the odds of finding one guy in all those woods are pretty small."

The navigator and I agreed on the target area and I rolled in to fire. I fired a one second burst just to check the guns. Before I could fire again we got a call from the ground.

"Great shooting Spooky! You can stop firing now. He just fell out of the tree!"

Now there is a case of someone not having a good night. There were thousands of other places that guy could have been, but he was right in the spot I chose to check my guns. I've never forgotten that moment over there. We orbited the camp for the next two hours and then flew home.

The next week, Colonel Swigler called for a Squadron Meeting. The flight commanders from all the other flights were there and Swigler dropped a bombshell on us.

"Men, the AC-47 Program, as far as the United States Air

Force is concerned, is coming to an end. On December 1 we are turning this mission and all our airplanes over to the South Vietnamese Air Force!"

We were all so stunned you could have heard a pin drop in the room. Swigler went on to say, "Some of you, with just a couple of months left to serve, will be going home early." A great cheer erupted in the room.

He continued, "And some of you will be reassigned to other units." A loud chorus of boos ensued.

There were some other housekeeping items and Colonel Swigler saved the best for last.

"I would like to congratulate Captain Trahan and Alpha Flight. Yours is the best combat readiness and effectiveness record in the Squadron for this quarter! Well done men!"

My flight cheered. I was so proud, because we had achieved what we said we would do. We were the best flight in the Squadron, at least for that reporting period. And now it looked like we would hold that record forever, because we were all being disbanded.

One last comment about Lt Colonel Adam Swigler: He and I didn't always agree, but I always disagreed with him respectfully. He showed a lot of confidence in me by letting me have command of that flight. I was fortunate to have that experience, because it is rare for a "first term" officer to get an opportunity like that, and especially one who was getting out of the Air Force at the end of his tour.

Adam never said much about our move from Nha Trang to Phan Rang, because my flight and I just made it happen as he told us to. Actually it was quite an ambitious undertaking to do that in the middle of a combat zone and we pulled it off. I didn't know how Swigler felt about it until I was notified that he had recommended me and I had been awarded the Air Force Commendation Medal for my role in that move and for taking over the fight with such effectiveness.

We had just ten days left in our Spooky Mission and I wanted to make the most of it for the younger pilots. Several of our copilots had not been there long enough to be in the Aircraft Commander upgrade syllabus so most of them had never fired the guns, except on gunnery training missions over the water. They had not fired them in combat.

For the rest of my missions I put my copilots in the left seat and let them have at it. I don't think there was anything better that I could have done for them.

Flight Log: November 28, 1969
Spooky 41   TIC Mission
AC: Captain Mike Trahan
CP: Lt Jim Popovich
Time: 2+10   16,500 Rounds 24 Flares

I put Jim in the left seat for this mission. I thought we would just go up and fly around for a few hours and land. This was the last night the USAF would be flying the Spooky Mission. We were turning the airplanes over to the Vietnamese in two days.

We were called out for a troops-in-contact mission and Jim did a great job. It was his one and only chance to fire the guns in a TIC mission. We landed and reloaded ammunition. I got in the left seat for the second flight that night.

Flight Log: November 29, 1969
Spooky 41 Regeneration   Last Spooky Mission

AC: Captain Mike Trahan
CP: Lt Jim Popovich
Time: 2+40   6,000 Rounds 24 Flares

We were called out on another TIC mission after our second takeoff. They mostly needed flare support so we provided that for them. Before we left the area I said, "Hey guys, this is our last Spooky flight. Are you sure you don't have something that needs to be shot up down there?"

The guy on the ground laughed and said, "Roger Spooky, understand you need to clear your guns one last time. How about some putting some suppressing fire on these coordinates? We have our suspicions about that area."

I rolled in and fired all three guns at fast rate, in sort of a farewell salute! When we called departing the area the guy on the ground said, "Thanks for all your great work Spooky. We are going to miss having you guys up there. You have saved our butts more times than we can count. Alpha Mike Fox!"

Swigler taxiing in on last Spooky flight

Colonel Swigler wanted the honor of making the last Spooky landing, so we came in to land first. And, wouldn't you know it, we had a problem with the landing gear and had to go around.

I called Swigler and said, "Sir we are going to have to go out and manually lower our landing gear. When we come back to land I will go to the end of the runway and park in one of our remote bunkers there."

That way he could land and taxi up to the designated place where the "Last Spooky Mission" was supposed to park. The press was there and there was a big celebration. Meanwhile, my crew and I quietly made the "real" last Spooky landing unnoticed and unheralded by anyone but us.

I am a firm believer of the Commandment "Thou shalt not kill!" It is one I never thought I would ever come close to violating in my life. I certainly had no desire to take a human life and yet, due to the circumstances of this assignment to the AC-47, I have taken hundreds of them. I never added up all the KBA reports, but I conservatively estimate that we killed over four hundred men during the one hundred missions I flew in the AC-47 program. When someone asks me how I feel about that I reply that I feel justified, because every person I took out was trying to kill American troops or those of our allies. I have never lost a minute's sleep over it.

Chapter 16

The EC-47 Electronic Countermeasures Aircraft

After we got the word that the AC-47 program was phasing out, everyone started speculating on what kind of assignment we would get. Would we be going home early or to another base in country or to one out of country? My assignment changed twice before it settled down to the final one. First I was going to go home early. I liked that one best. Then I was going to be a Base Operations officer in Korea. That sounded okay with me. At least I would be out of this lousy war.

The third assignment stuck. I was going to Pleiku to fly the EC-47 with the 362nd Tactical Electronic Warfare Squadron. The EC-47 didn't carry any guns, so I was right back where I was in the C-141 - flying around in a war zone, getting shot at, and I couldn't shoot back!

Jim Popovich went to Korea and Jamie Little went to the 362nd with me. However, Jamie got a serious eye infection right after he arrived in Pleiku and he went home early. I don't remember where the other pilots from my flight went. I believe they went home.

I arrived in Pleiku right before Christmas. My welcome was warm enough but I was in for another disappointment. The Flight Commander and Operations Officer both knew that I had come from the AC-47 and that I was a qualified Instructor Pilot in that aircraft. That didn't cut any ice with them. I would still have to fly right seat until I was checked out in the EC-47 Mission.

I could not believe it. As far as the Aircraft Commander was concerned, the EC-47 mission consisted entirely of flying the headings the navigator gave him. How damned hard could that be?

They asked me if I was interested in any extra duty assignments and I said, unless they needed me for one, I would just as soon pass. I told them I was getting out of the Air Force in four months and I certainly didn't need any more stuff to put on my resume.

They said, "Okay Mike, we will fly you every other day. Aside from that you are free to do what you wish."

That sounded great to me. I was paired with Lieutenant Colonel Vizzini for seven rides in the right seat. I thought that was about six rides too many but there was nothing I could do about it.

On January 11, I left for Hawaii and a glorious week of R&R with Sheila. I've never seen her looking more beautiful than she did when she met my flight that day.

We stayed at the Outrigger Hotel right on Waikiki beach and we spent our days exploring Oahu and eating some of the best food I've ever tasted. We talked a lot about Theresa, who was staying with my parents while Sheila was in Hawaii. She told me about all the cute and wonderful things Theresa did during the nine months I was away from home.

We also discussed our future plans, hopes, and dreams. We knew that my getting out of the Air Force was taking a big chance. I would be unemployed, when I arrived back in the United States, and finding an airline job was not a guaranteed thing. On one of my trips to Taiwan I bought a book that contained the addresses of every airline in the free world, and I had written to every one of them and requested an employment application. I told Sheila I was aggressively pursuing a job and hoped to have some interviews lined up by the time I got home. She was pleased to hear that.

Our week together flew by and before we knew it, it was time for me to head back to Vietnam. This goodbye was even harder than when I left San Angelo to begin my tour. However, Sheila and I knew I would be home in just a little more than three months and we knew we could handle that. That anxiety about having to leave R&R and go back stayed with me for years. My only "Nam Flashback" was a recurring dream that I had not finished my tour in Vietnam and the Air Force made me go back and do that.

At a Luau during R&R

As soon as I got back to the Squadron they set me up for my Aircraft Commander Check out. I got three left seat rides and a check ride. All went well with the check ride and on January 30, 1970 I was qualified as an EC-47 Aircraft Commander.

I flew twenty-one more missions in the EC-47 and I have to say that they were boring as hell and they were long. They lasted anywhere from five to seven hours. We were just a flying platform for some intelligence gathering personnel. There were several stations in the cabin where men would sit monitoring some ground tracking devices that had been placed by Special Forces. I didn't really know all they did back there and I didn't want to know. All I had to do was fly the headings and tracks the navigator gave me.

My EC-47 Crew: Me, McNabb, Passey and Funk

However, I must say this about the EC-47 mission. It was one of the most DANGEROUS missions over there! We flew this antique twin-engine airplane at one hundred thirty knots, at three thousand feet, in broad daylight, over some of the most hostile real estate in Vietnam and Laos. Some missions had us flying up and down the treacherous Ho Chi Minh trail all day long.

I believe the concept, according to headquarters PACAF, was this: The enemy would assume ours was a cargo airplane and rather than give away their positions to shoot us down, they would leave us alone. Well, that concept was messed up!

One day we were flying along the Ho Chi Minh trail. We were flying a triangular pattern and we kept turning at the same places again and again and again. I commented to the navigator and the copilot that this was not wise.

"Cargo airplanes didn't fly these kinds patterns for hours on end. They fly a straight line from point to point. Sooner or later those bad guys down there are going to realize that this is not a cargo airplane, and when they do, somebody is going to get shot down. And it's going to happen right here."

When we landed I reported my concerns to my Flight Commander and the Intelligence Officer. Apparently my comments fell on deaf ears, because two weeks after I left Vietnam an EC-47 was shot down exactly where I said it would happen. Lt. Mike Wall, the aircraft commander, was killed in the crash. I liked Mike. He was an Ole Miss graduate, so that gave us a lot in common. This was his first assignment right out of pilot training.

In a strange twist of fate, the copilot who was flying with me the day I made that prediction, was flying with Wall when they got shot down. I don't remember his first name because we had a nickname for him. His last name was Nastipak, so naturally we called him "Nasty." I wonder if Nasty remembered my prediction when they started taking ground fire that day!

Mike Wall (leaning on fence) Killed in Action

I remember that, during our flight together, Nastipak took a grease pencil and wrote "Y Me God?" on the windshield in front of him. In that crash he went through that same windshield. It didn't kill him but it sure scalped him.

That story reminds me of another notable mission. It happened on my EC-47 Aircraft Commander Tactical Check ride. Lt. Colonel Wells was the Flight Examiner.

We were working near the DMZ and we got a message from one of the station operators in the back of the airplane. He said PACAF wanted us to go fly in an area NORTH of the DMZ. That, my friends, is in North Vietnam! None of the EC-

47s was flying north at that time, nor had they ever as far as I know. It would have been suicide.

I told the crew we were not doing anything until I got that order verified. The navigator called our Command Post and asked them to confirm their order that we were supposed to go fly in that area.

The Command Post came back and said, "Negative, negative, negative! That message was telling you to AVOID that area at all costs, due to the high SAM threat there." A SAM is a surface to air missile. The airman who miss-interpreted that message got so upset he hyperventilated and passed out.

Of the three places where I was based during my year in Vietnam, Pleiku was my favorite. It was located in the central highlands and because of its higher field elevation Pleiku was a lot cooler than Nha Trang and Phan Rang, which were at sea level. In fact, it got so cool at night we could turn off our air conditioners and still have to use a light blanket. I preferred to sleep with the air conditioner off. I wanted to hear what was going on around there.

Pleiku was known around Vietnam as "Rocket City!" It got that name because it had received so many rocket attacks. Earlier I mentioned that Pleiku was always surrounded by enemy troops and that remained true the entire time I was there. We had a rocket attack during my last night at Pleiku. But I am getting ahead of myself.

One of my most vivid memories of Pleiku was Christmas Eve. I tried to go to Midnight Mass but it was so crowded when I arrived people were already standing outside the chapel. I decided to skip that Mass and go on Christmas morning.

I walked up a hill to the highest point on the base and stood there looking at a star-filled sky. I thought about where I was and what I had been doing the past nine months and I wept. I wept for Sheila and Theresa who had to endure my being gone so long. I wept for my parents, who were not getting any younger, and who were sick with worry that their only son might not make it back home. I wept for myself, because this we not where I wanted to be on Christmas Eve. But most of all I wept for the people of Vietnam. I had been up and down and sideways across South Vietnam and I had seen first hand the devastation this war had wrought on that beautiful country. I was just so overwhelmingly sad for them.

Flight Log: February 20 & 21, 1970
Ferry Flight – Taking an aircraft to Taiwan
AC: Captain Mike Trahan
Copilot: Joel Owens
Navigators: Villafranco and Jacobson
Pleiku to Clark AFB, PI   Time: 5+45
Clark to Tai Chung, Taiwan   Time: 4+0

We left early on the morning of February 20 and flew to Clark Air Force Base in the Philippines. We spent the night at Clark and then flew up to Tai Chung the next day.

When we got to Tai Chung I called my Flight Commander back in Pleiku.

"Sir, we are here and the airplane is delivered. When do you want us to come back to Pleiku?"

"What do your orders say Mike?"

I told him they gave us a return date of 28 February.

"Then I don't want to see you before that date. You guys enjoy your little vacation on us. You deserve it!" And that is what we did.

On the 27th I went into the office of Lieutenant Colonel Boyd. He was the commander of a C-130 unit there at Tai Chung. I hit him up for a ride back to Pleiku on the 28th for my crew and myself. He said he would be glad to accommodate us.

When I was in his office I noticed a picture of Hopalong Cassidy hanging on his wall. I knew that Cassidy's real name was William Boyd. I just had to ask.

"Colonel Boyd, would you happen to be kin to Ole Hopalong up there?"

He smiled, puffed out his chest in pride and said, "Yep, he's my brother!"

I told him about all those old cowboy movies I watched as a kid. He said, "I watched the same ones Mike."

With Dick Burkhead and Ben Alford

Celebrating after our Last Mission

DEROS was the Air Force acronym for Date of Return from Overseas. My DEROS was April 6, 1970. My last flight in Vietnam, and in the Air Force for that matter, took place on March 30, 1970.

Flight Log: March 30, 1970
AC: Captain Mike Trahan
Copilot: Lt Ben Alford
Navigator: Marshall Goodwin
Time: 7+0

There were many milestones connected with this flight. It was my last combat mission in Vietnam and it was my last flight as an Air Force pilot. My commitment to the USAF had been completed and I would be getting out in less than a week. All that was weighing on my mind as we approached Pleiku for that last landing.

There is no describing the relief I felt when this mission was over. I had just flown the last seven of my four hundred and eighty five hours of combat time in Vietnam. This was combat sortie number one hundred thirty one for me and, by the grace of God I had survived them all without a scratch. Thanks be to Him!

Ben Alford was my copilot on this flight. It was his last flight too. Dick Burkhead flew his last mission at the same time I did. We joined up and flew formation back to the field after our missions were finished. He landed first and I made a low pass with a pull up to a closed pattern for my last approach and landing. Dick, Ben and I met at the Officer's Club that evening and celebrated with more than a couple of drinks. Burkhead and I wound up on the same airline seniority list a couple of years later.

I spent three more days in Pleiku after that last mission. Most of that time was spent out processing from the Squadron and turning in all my Air Force gear. I was able to keep my used flight suits and boots, but the other gear had to go back. It was just as well. I had no need for it.

On my last night in Pleiku we had an attack on the base. The enemy had lobbed a couple of rockets into the base and word came around that there might have been a breach of the perimeter and some bad guys had gotten on the base. I had my M-16 locked and loaded, my flak jacket and combat helmet on, and I was crouched behind a brick revetment wall that surrounded out Bachelor Officer's Quarters. Dick Burkhead, Jay Fansler, and Ben Alford were there with me.

I commented, "I've spent three hundred and sixty days in Vietnam, and now here on my last night in Pleiku, I have to assume the role of a grunt soldier. Hell, I don't know how to be a foot soldier – but, by God, I do know how to shoot!"

Fortunately we didn't see any bad guys coming across the fence.

The next day Burkhead, Alford, and I flew down to Cam Ranh Bay to be in position to catch our Freedom Bird home on April 6. I don't remember what I did during those three days. It is all blurry now. I do remember being very edgy for some reason. I had heard horror stories of men who were killed on their last day in Vietnam, while waiting for their flight home. I think I prayed a lot!

Before I end this I have to share one funny tradition we

had in Vietnam. Everyone was there for a one-year tour, unless they were flying missions into North Vietnam. In that case they went home after completing 100 missions up there. Each mission north was called a "Counter."

No matter what the method of countdown, we all had our "Short" Calendars. It was usually a picture of a beautiful shapely nude woman and it was divided into 365 or 100 little sections. As you served each day or flew each counter you filled in that section. I don't think I have to tell you where the last little section was!

Some guys also liked to write how many days they had left on the latrine walls. They usually wrote, "Short, only twenty days to go!" or "Short, only ten counters to go!" But the funniest one I ever saw was this, "Short, only 10,786 days to go!" Someone wrote, "Why so long?" Under that was written, "Because I'm Vietnamese dammit!"

One day I was walking along the sidewalk at Cam Ranh Bay and this airman walked by. He saluted me and when I returned his salute I made the sign of the cross instead of just dropping my hand by my side. That should give you some indication about my frame of mind at the time.

Our Freedom Bird was a Continental Military Charter Boeing 707. We made a brief fueling stop at Yokota Air Base and we were on our way to the good old USA. I don't remember if we went nonstop to McChord AFB in Washington, or if we stopped in Anchorage. All I remember is that we landed around seven in the morning. I had orders to go right to outprocessing and complete the paperwork to get out of the Air Force. I also had to take an exit physical.

It was after 0800 when I got there and an airman clerk

said, "Sorry Captain, but you will have to come back tomorrow. We don't out-process anyone who gets here after 0800." I told him he had better damn well let me out-process right then or I was going to kick his ass. His boss, a Major, heard the commotion and came into the room. He took one look at the rage on my face and said, "I think it would be best if you go ahead and let Captain Trahan out of the Air Force today."

As soon as I could get to a telephone I called Sheila and told her I was back in the USA. I could hear the relief in her voice all the way from Texas to Washington State. I told her it would be another two days before I got home. I would be arriving in Dallas too late the next day to catch the San Angelo flight. She offered to drive to Dallas and meet me and I advised against it. I said I was going to be pretty exhausted when I landed in Dallas and it would be better to just wait in San Angelo.

My second call went to Mom and Dad. They were so happy to hear my voice and I was so happy to hear theirs. They said they would drive to San Angelo the next day and meet me when I landed.

My third call went to Victor Moreau in Alexandria, Louisiana. Vic let me stay in his garage apartment during my AC-47 training, and the only payment he wanted was for me to come back home alive. I promised I would call him when I got back and I did.

My flight to Texas was scheduled to depart Seattle at six pm the next day. We were bussed to the terminal at Seattle Tacoma Airport. When we got off the bus the war protesters were there to greet us. They spat at us and called us baby killers. It was not the reception I expected to get but it was what it was. I've always thought it so ironic that the people who called me a baby killer that day are now the ones who are the biggest proponents of abortion.

Our takeoff from Seattle was on time, and as we climbed out and made our turn eastbound my window was filled with a magnificent view of Mount Rainer bathed in the golden glow of sunset. It was a very memorable moment for me.

We landed in Dallas after nine o'clock, so I got a room in a cheap hotel across the street from Love Field. I was so exhausted I fell asleep immediately.

The next morning I caught the first flight to San Angelo. When I stepped off the airplane I was greeted by my beautiful wife Sheila, our now two-year old daughter Theresa and my Mother and Dad. I looked up and said a prayer of thanksgiving. Then I embraced them all. The next chapter of my life had just begun!

ACKNOWLEDGEMENTS

I would like to recognize the following people, for their contributions to this book. Were it not for their efforts, it never would have seen the light of day.

Thank you: To my wife, Sheila, for giving me the time, space, and support I needed while I was writing this book.

Thank you: To my fellow pilot and friend Becky McLendon, for the wonderful job she did proofreading and editing this book.

Thank You: To my friend, Fred Hubbard, for his expert advice on my Macintosh Computer, and for providing the template I use to format my books.

And, last but not least, thank you to, Nick Wale of William Collins Publishing and Novel Ideas, for producing my books and then presenting them to readers all over the world.

ABOUT THE AUTHOR

Mike Trahan

Mike Trahan grew up in West Orange, Texas, and, at age fifteen, he started taking flying lessons. He flew light aircraft during high school and college, and by the time he entered Air Force Pilot Training, he had accumulated 650 hours of flying time and a Commercial Pilot Certificate with single and multi-engine ratings.

Mike spent four and a half years in the U.S .Air Force. As an Air Force pilot, he flew C-141 jet transports out of Charleston, S.C. and AC-47 "Spooky" Gunships and EC-47 air-craft in Vietnam. By the time he left the Air Force, he had accumulated 3400 flight hours.

After resigning from the Air Force, Mike was hired by Delta Air Lines. While with Delta, he flew the Convair 880, Douglas DC-9 and Boeing 727, 737, 757 and 767 aircraft. He retired at age sixty, in 2002, after thirty-two years with Delta. Mike acquired over 20,000 flight hours during his forty-five year flying career.

Mike and Sheila have three children: Theresa, Jim, and

Jerry. Two granddaughters: Jordan Nicole and Hazel Grace. And two great-granddaughters: Sevyn Sadie and Dylan.

Other Books by Mike Trahan

"The Gift – The Beginning"

"The Gift – The Delta Years"

43208928R00181